Wildflower Girl

By Dana Stewart Quinney

Hidden Shelf Publishing House
P.O. Box 4168, McCall, ID 83638
www.hiddenshelfpublishinghouse.com

Cover photo: Dana Quinney as a child

Graphic design: Allison Kaukola (back cover),
Kristen Carrico (front cover)

Interior layout: Kerstin Stokes

Editor: Carol Anne Wagner

Library of Congress Cataloguing-in-Publication Data

Quinney, Dana Stewart
Wildflower Girl

ISBN: 978-1-7338193-0-5

Printed in the United States of America

WILDFLOWER GIRL

"When Dana was three years old, she mastered a somersault, a monumental time in her young life. She wanted to remember that somersault forever, and her Mom taught her a way. She applied the same method toward remembering all the important events in her life. They are assembled together in this captivating compilation of short stories. Travel with Danny through these magical times as she witnesses a murder (or did she?) from her secret watching place, finds the stars with her adventuresome father, and almost loses her life in her grandpa's waders. And, always the botanist and biologist, twenty years after Danny's grandpa told her that "all of the animals isn't all found out" she discovers a new species of Fairy Shrimp. I became lost in these fascinating stories."
    — Carol Howell, Jade Mist Shetland Sheepdogs

"This lovely book of short stories is like a portal, taking the reader back to a simpler, more innocent time in a magical place. It is a place that was real, but unavailable to anyone in today's world, unless you allow this book to take you there. The author's descriptions are crisp and clear. You are taken on one adventure after another in a most vivid and delightful way and introduced to some amazing characters. Whether or not you are familiar with the area and the time, you have a clear view of her world and her life. I am so thankful for the memories stirred to life by the author's stories."
    — Margaret "Mib" Brown Kelly, childhood friend in Ketchum, Idaho

"In Wildflower Girl, Dana has gifted us with glimpses of a childhood that was often magical, without losing sight of some of the hard truths of learning about life in general. She is a gifted storyteller and the memories of this time and place are so well crafted that the reader can see the stories and feel the emotions. Thanks to Dana for the invitation into these experiences; I'm sure I am not the only one who will revisit frequently."
    — Lisa Butterfield, Windanseur Arabians

List of Stories

Introduction

When I was small, I set out to find treasure. I'm a finder, you see. We finders find things. A horse, a dog, a field guide, a book of poetry, a notebook, a packed lunch: these were my tools of discovery. I found white buttercups in the snow of the Fourhills above our house, shining trout in beaver ponds, silver-marked butterflies near the mouth of an old mine, strange creatures and stranger flowers in the far places of the world, and above all, I found stories.

The Fourhills of Ketchum, Idaho led me into a life filled with creatures and flowers, fish, and trees, wonder and awe—all the things experienced by an outdoor biologist as she searches the world for her kind of treasure. Since you are holding this book in your hands, I know that you are a finder, too. Welcome to my world of little lives.

To my parents, Bernice Stewart
and Clayton "Stew" Stewart.

Me at age 4 in my grandmother Lily's garden.

The Purple Glass Pitcher

"You cannot remember that much detail after so long a time," people tell me. "You cannot remember what it's like to be three years old when you are 70. You cannot remember what you were wearing, what clouds were in the sky, what your mother said, how your puppy's bark sounded. That's not possible."

But I can and it is.

I don't remember everything, of course. Just as you have, I have forgotten countless things, countless people, countless happenings. But there are some things I remember with a crystalline clarity, all because of my mother.

I was three and a half years old, and on a blustery gray November morning, I got dressed in navy corduroy overalls, a green blouse, and my brown-and-gold checked wool coat, the one with the brown velvet collar and the silver buttons that looked like little flowers. Mom was busy ironing and sent me out to play in the yard.

As always at over 6,000 feet, the November grass was crisp, pale, and dormant. A cold wind blew down from the Fourhills. Mom tucked the back-end triangle of my yellow headscarf into my coat collar, and I toddled out into the front yard.

Our yard was raised about three feet from the dirt road that went up the hill past our house, and on two sides, the yard had a bank, a short, steep slope down to the road on one side and down to the driveway on the other. This little slope was perfect for me to slide down on the seat of my pants (grass stains) or roll down, over and over (more grass stains). But today, this little blonde girl in the tidy braids had a mission, something much more exciting than rolling four feet down a grassy bank onto the edge of a dirt driveway.

I had seen one of the big boys in the neighborhood, Jimmy Campbell, do a somersault. In fact, I had watched Jimmy do several somersaults, and I had been thinking about them for a day or two. Today I was going to do a somersault.

Jimmy had put his head right down on the grass, yep. I did that and kicked my legs a little, as I had seen Jimmy do.

I fell over to one side.

I did it again. I fell over to one side. By this time I wasn't paying much attention to where I was, and my scrabbling around on the grass had brought me to the edge of the steep little bank.

Gritting my teeth, I put my head down once more on the cold grass. Bracing with my arms, I kicked up, trying to stay straight. And I did a headstand, my first! But, because I was right on the edge of the bank, I tumbled over and somersaulted down the bank!

Whoa! This knocked the breath right out of my small lungs. But because I had tumbled down the bank as well as doing my first somersault, this was big. Very big, for someone not yet four years old. I scrambled up the bank and did it again. Whoof! And again.

At this point, I had to tell Mom. I rushed into the house, breathless. Then I tugged at Mom's hand until she put down the iron and came outside into the icy wind to see me do a silly, tumbling-down somersault. We both laughed, and then ran back inside.

Mom picked up the iron. She was ironing my favorite dress, a light blue cotton dress with ruffled sleeves, printed all over with blue and yellow butterflies.

"I want to remember that forever!" I told her. "Forever and ever. "I looked out the window for a moment, at the bare aspens down at Coats's house bending in the wind.

Even at that age, I knew that I forgot things. But this I wanted to keep. "Mommy, how can I remember this forever and ever?" I asked her.

Mom put down the iron again and pushed back her hair. "Well, here's how, Danny," she told me. I stared at her; she wasn't joking.

She went on. "I know you can count to five. On the first day, you think of it five different times. Each time, you think of what you did, what you saw, what you smelled, what you touched, what you felt inside, if it was cold or hot, what you were wearing, and what you were thinking."

I nodded eagerly. "Five times," I said.

"Then the next day, you think of it five times again." Mom picked up the iron. "For a week, you think of it every day, five times. Then for a month, you think of it once a day, and five times on a certain day in that week. Do you know what a month is?"

"A month is four weeks, and the months have names," I said. "November, December. And April, where my birthday is."

"That's right," Mom said. "You can watch for when we change the page on the Union Pacific calendar in the kitchen, and look for the same day as today in the next month. That will be December."

"OK," I said. "Then what?"

"Then you think of it one time a month for a year."

I took a moment to digest this. "What do I do after a year?" I could hardly imagine a whole year.

Mom laughed. "Then any time, just before you go to sleep, you can call the memory, and it will come, and it will follow you to sleep."

9

"Can you remember anything this way?" I asked.

"Anything."

"Oh, boy," I said, determined. "I will sit here right now and do my five thinks for today before I forget."

Mom chuckled and went back to her ironing.

Several months later, in late April, my friend AnnaMary came over to play. Our mothers were friends, and once in a while, one mom would drop her girl off at the other one's house to play so that the mom could do some errands.

On this bright and breezy afternoon, the snowmelt-mud of the soil on the Fourhills had recently dried after a long winter, and early wildflowers dotted the slopes, hiding in the sage.

As the two of us stood on the driveway watching the dust of AnnaMary's family car trail down the hill, AnnaMary and I decided to go climbing.

For a four-year-old, this meant going up our road a short way, walking a hundred feet through sage and wild rye, and busying ourselves in a small, angular outcrop of pinkish rock, parts of it jagged, and other areas hollowed with slick, curved sides as if they had been dug out with a twist of an oversized ice-cream scoop.

These little scoops in the bedrock, about half as long as we were tall, we found perfect for climbing on and sliding down. We watched our feet carefully in the broken rock, because when you are four, where you put your feet is a matter for concentration.

Something glinted there in the rock, something bright and shiny. I saw it first, because even then, I was a finder.

I reached into a little nook of dirt and moss, and my chubby fingers closed upon the handle of a small glass pitcher. I pulled it out and held it up.

I now know that my prize was a pressed-glass or cut-glass cream pitcher, but then it seemed like a treasure made of diamonds. 'Look, AnnaMary!" I cried, scrambling down into a scooped-out place in the rock. "Look what I found! And it's purple. Purple!"

Purple glass was very likely not significant to little AnnaMary, but even at four years old, I knew it was something special. My parents had told me that old glass, very old glass, turned purple after many years in the sun. Newer glass stayed colorless. This meant that purple glass was something left by, or lost by, the pioneers.

My parents and grandparents always spoke of pioneers with a kind of hushed awe. "They came out here in covered wagons," Gramps would say, "hoping for a new life. They carried seeds and some tools. It wasn't easy, and not all of them made it. Some of them froze to death or drowned in river crossings. Some were killed by Indians. Some got sick on the way and were buried beside the trail. And some died in accidents with their wagons and horses."

I knew that pioneers were brave and clever, the ones like my great-grandparents, who had made it to Idaho and Utah. And anything belonging to them was precious. My parents, coming upon an old cabin, or a place in the sage where glass fragments lay shining on the ground, would search for purple bottles. When they happened to find a purple bottle unbroken, they took it home, washed and dried it carefully, and placed it on display in the glass-fronted wall cabinet that Dad had found at the dump-ground north of town.

And I had found a purple bottle all by myself—only this was not just a plain old bottle, but a gorgeous, glorious, perfect little pitcher!

I began to walk down the hill. I had to show this to my mom! At last I would have something to go into the special wall cabinet.

But fate had other plans, in the form of spoiled little AnnaMary. "Give it to me!" she demanded, reaching for the pitcher. "I'm the guest, so you should give it to me. I saw it

My mother and me in 1947. The purple glass pitcher was found in the rocks on the hill in the middle of the photo.

first!"

I knew she hadn't seen it first. The pitcher was mine.

As AnnaMary grabbed for it, I lifted the pitcher high over my head. She charged me, wrenched it away from my hand, and—it fell.

The pitcher fell on the rocks.

Frozen in my tracks, I was devastated. The pitcher was not merely broken, it was shattered, shattered into too many pieces ever to be glued back together.

My face felt hot, and the hillside went wavery as the tears came.

"Serves you right," AnnaMary was saying, singsong. "Serves you right, serves you right, serves you right. It's your fault the pitcher broke, Danny. You went and broke it."

I ignored her. A pioneer's pitcher—loved so much that it had been carried all the way from the East in a covered wagon—now gone forever. I heard myself sobbing.

Heedless, I ran down the hill and into our backyard. When I burst into the house crying, Mom was in the kitchen making an apple pie. She took me into her lap and dried my tears.

Eventually Mother got AnnaMary and me calmed down. She brought out crayons and two of my coloring books.

Lying on the living-room floor, AnnaMary and I colored in silence. I didn't want to play with AnnaMary anymore, and I felt good when her mother came for her an hour later.

After AnnaMary had gone, Mother asked me to tell her exactly what had happened. I broke into tears again. I couldn't bear to think of the beautiful pitcher now in fragments in the rocks. I had wanted so much, so very much, to keep it forever because it was beautiful and because of the pioneers.

Mom's face was grave, and fishing out her damp handkerchief once more, she sat me down in a kitchen chair. After drying my tears a second time, she pulled her chair close to mine, so we were sitting knees to knees.

13

She said, "Danny, do you know how you can keep that pitcher forever?" She stared earnestly into my face.

"It's broken!" I gulped, again on the verge of tears.

"Think," she said. "How can you have that pitcher for always?"

I gulped again, but then the light came on. "Think—think of it five times today," I said, sniffling.

She clapped her hands. "Yes! That is exactly right! Think of the pitcher before it was broken. Think of it five times today. And then—" she paused.

"Think of it five times every day for a week!" I said in triumph. I felt as if the sun had come out from behind the clouds.

"And then think of it once a week for a month, and five times on a certain day in each week!" we said together.

Seventy years have gone by, and I still have the little purple pitcher. I can see it now, sparkling on the rusty green star-moss at the edge of the pinkish rock outcrop there on the Fourhills, lying where some pioneer had lost it, or placed it for safekeeping.

I see the pink andesite of the rock and the shining faceted glass in the dirt at the foot of the little slide-scoop, and the star moss that grew in the cracks of the rocks, and the red corduroy pants I had on, and how a big bird's shadow had passed over me just before I bent to take the purple glass handle, and I smell the spicy scent of the wild-parsnip with its many brown flowers. I see the silvery undersides of the lupine leaves bowing in the spring breeze, and my small Buster Brown shoes with their floppy laces, and the red-and-black ants marching up the rock slide. The wind lifts my bangs and I hold the pitcher up to the sun. Below, a short way down our dirt road, I see the roof of our house, covered in green shingles, and our trees.

Yet, there's more.

Mom passed away in 1983. I still miss her so much that it

hurts. But sometimes I see her.

To this day, as part of the purple pitcher's remembering, just for a moment I have Mom at age 28, her luxuriant blonde hair held back on one side with a tortoiseshell barrette. She is leaning toward me holding a crumpled white handkerchief in one hand. I see her vivid blue eyes and full lips, the yellow apron over the white blouse and navy blue pleated slacks she wore that day, her hands floury from making pie crust, our puppy Angrynuff curled at her feet, the warm air in the kitchen fragrant with the scent of cinnamon. And I see the green glass bowl filled with sliced apples—the last of the winter apples that had been stored in our root cellar—sitting on the white-painted table that Gramps had made, and a wooden rolling pin and two tin pie plates there as well. I see Mom's smile and the expression in her eyes, and once again I hold in my heart the warmth of belonging, of being cherished—the feeling of all things being just right. I remember.

The Finder and the Pool of Gold

When I was small, I set out to find treasure, and this is the story of what I found. When you are little, very small things seem large. That doesn't make them any less real.

I was five years old. It was a brisk, windy morning in early spring, a day of broken overcast and trickling snowmelt. The lawn at Mom and Gramps' house in Ketchum was patchy brown and yellow, and as yet there were no buds on the spruce trees. A few daffodil spears poked from the ground. More than two weeks would pass before there would be flowers. The sky was gray and the wind was cold; Mother said that the air came straight down the valley from the mountains still deep in snow.

Mother and grandmother (who was affectionately known in the family as "Moms") were having coffee at Moms and Gramps' house. I was tired of being indoors, and buttoned on my brown-checked wool coat. "I'm going out to find some treasure," I announced to the two women, pretending that I didn't notice their smiles. They might doubt, but I thought I could very well find some treasure.

Gramps had told me that if you didn't look, you would never find. He said that he was a finder, and he wondered if I was one. So I was going to look to see if I could find. Now, older than Gramps was then, I know that Gramps was right. People are of two kinds: finders and non-finders. I'm a finder.

I clumped down Moms' wooden porch steps and stepped

16

into the cold air. The wind took my long braids and danced them wildly until I stuffed them down my coat collar.

Moms and Gramps' front yard was small and familiar, bounded on one side by their house itself and on the other with a line of spruce. At the northwest end of the yard was Moms' rock garden, a tiered affair with pockets of soil that held pansies every summer, built around and culminating in a natural rock outcrop of pink rhyolite. Beyond the rock garden was an empty lot, and beyond that, the Fourhills, small hills beloved of the children in our part of the town of Ketchum. I soon left the yard; everything here was still asleep from the winter. The empty lot beckoned.

Nothing had ever been built on the empty lot between Moms and Gramps' house and the Fourhills. Beside a few low out-crops of the rhyolite, the ground was covered with sagebrush, wild bunchgrasses flattened by the heavy winter snows that had so recently melted, and little green nubs here and there that soon would grow into wildflowers. Between the plants there was cold mud. I began to walk in little circles, eyes on the ground, looking for treasure. I was certain that I would find treasure, if I spent enough time looking.

Near one of the small rock outcrops, what I did find were ants. These were very tiny, non-aggressive tan fellows who made inch-high volcanoes of sand grains as the entrances to their nests. From the height of an adult person, these tiny ants are invisible and their colonies barely noticeable. From the height of a five-year-old, the colonies are obvious and interest-ing.

Still, these particular ants themselves are exceedingly small. While I was standing up, it was difficult to see what they were doing. Carefully, I lay on my stomach in the mud and watched them.

The ants were carrying grains of something in their jaws, and most of the ants going into the volcano hole had such grains. Most of the ants coming out of the volcano hole held nothing. So, they were gathering something and taking it home. I was very pleased when I figured that out. After a few minutes, I noticed that some of the ants coming out of the hole were each carrying a large, blocky brown object. Wait! These brown things were not something they carried. I was startled to discover that the blocky brown objects were their heads! These ants were different. They had huge heads and huge jaws. But—these were living peacefully in the same volcano as the smaller ants with ordinary heads. And the big-headed ones were not carrying anything. I took up a sage twig and poked gently at the volcano.

Suddenly a dozen of the big-headed ants boiled from the volcano hole and attacked the stick! I laid the stick down and watched these big-headed ants swarm over it, biting it with their oversized brown jaws. I had discovered for myself the ant-society system of castes, though it would be years later when I would read about it in a natural history book. However, even then I understood that these big ants were protectors of the smaller ones, watching for danger so the small ones could do their work. Later I would find that the big ones were called soldiers and the ordinary ones were called workers.

Inches behind the ant volcano, a plate-sized rock leaned at an angle against the face of the nearest rhyolite outcrop, creating a very small cave behind it. I had heard enough stories to know that pirates liked to hide treasure in caves. This was a very, very small cave. I thought it might be just right for a very, very small treasure.

Using my elbows and moving to one side of the ant colony, I hitched myself forward on my stomach until I could see into the rock cave. The ground was cold and the wetness of the mud began to seep through my wool coat, but I put that into the back of my mind. Like a little dog, I thrust my nose into the small opening as my eyes adjusted to the pocket of shadow behind the leaning rock.

And I found gold! Through the narrow crack where the leaning rock met the face of the outcrop, a beam of light sliced down onto the floor of the cave, and in that shaft of sunlight shone a pool of gold.

Even at five, I well knew what gold was: Mother's wedding ring, pictures of gold coins in storybooks, the shiny metallic buttons on Daddy's Navy uniform from the War, a nugget that Gramps kept in a small jar in his desk drawer. This was just the same, vivid and shiny like the purest metallic gold, except that this was melted into a pool of the size that might fit into my cupped hands. Unaccountably, a teaspoon of molten gold lay, treasure of unfathomable strangeness, inside my cave. And it was moving.

From the oval border of the golden pool, a projection that looked like a leg gathered and streamed away from the beam of sunlight. The rest of the pool followed, coming with the leg, as slowly as could be noticed. I bit my finger and tried to understand. The pool of gold was now in shadow. The projection relaxed into the pool, and once again the thing was a simple oval. The patch of blue in the cloud cover closed, and the beam of sunshine winked away, gone. Another leg came out from the golden pool, and the thing moved back to where it had been before.

"Melted things are hot," I thought. I knew about candles and melted wax. So I held my finger just above the pool for a count of ten and felt no heat. Then I dipped the finger and felt cool wetness. The pool divided into two away from my finger, and very slowly the halves each threw out a projection and made for the back of the cave. The two puddles coalesced into one as they reached deep shadow.

I remember thinking very hard as I studied the metallic golden sheen of the teaspoon-sized pool. What was this? The treasure couldn't be real gold, because it was liquid and cool, and liquid gold was melted metal and so had to be very hot. The treasure couldn't be real gold, because it moved, and not just downhill the way water moves; it was alive. And truly, if I were honest and did no make-believe at all, I knew that there were no pirates in Ketchum, Idaho, not even very small pirates. But this *was* a treasure. Wasn't it? I lay motionless, waiting for the pool of gold to move again.

Presently another projection nosed out, and the pool streamed across the floor of the cave and, defying gravity, flowed up the side of the rock outcrop, where it came to rest on the rough rhyolite, taking the shape of a long oval. The cold of the mud where I lay finally presented itself to the front of my mind, but I lay as still as I could for a long time.

The golden pool lay still, too. I thought about it, very hard. There were many stories in my books, and there were stories Mother told, about treasures. Most of these were treasures of gold coins and jewels. Some stories told about different treasures, like little gold statues or gold bars. One treasure was a single black pearl. There was even one story about a box of paper money that some boys found in an old house. That was a treasure, too. Treasures were rare and precious, not often found, things of great value. But this strange golden pool holding fast to the side of a rough rock here in the empty lot: was this really a treasure?

Before I could think more, I was up and running back to the house. I burst through the door, shouting, "Mommy, Mommy, come and look at this gold and tell me if it is a treasure!"

Mother smiled, amused, and set down her coffee cup. "What is it, Danny? What have you found?"

"Come on!" I cried, dragging at her hand. "You have to come and look. Please. I think I found a treasure!"

My grandmother smiled, but said sternly, "Oh, Danny, look at your pants. And your coat! You are mud all over. Did you fall down?"

The day I found the pool of gold.

"No," I said as calmly as I could, but my eyes were for Mother. "I didn't *fall* down."

Mother got to her feet slowly and reached for her jacket on the back of the chair. She looked out the window into the brown yard. The sun had come out again, and the sky was cloudy bright. "All, right, let's go see this treasure of yours."

I pulled her out the door, babbling in my excitement. "It's gold. I found gold! I think it's a treasure."

Mother allowed herself to be led through the yard and up to the rock outcrop in the empty lot.

"It's in there!" I said.

Mother looked at the little space between the rock and the outcrop. "It's in there? Let me just move this one rock."

"Oh, please don't do that!" I held her hand away, remembering how the golden pool had sought the shadows away from the sunlight. "I think it might be hurt if you move the rock."

"But if I don't move the rock I'll have to get down on the ground to see in," she said, hesitating. After a moment, she knelt in the mud and bent her face as close to the ground as I had. She looked into my little cave. "What does the treasure look like?"

"It's gold," I said. "I told you it was gold."

I waited impatiently, dancing from foot to foot.

Suddenly, Mother said, "Oh." She held still for what seemed a long time, and then she said, "I see it, Danny." Then she added, "It moves. It's moving. It's changing shape. Did you see it do that?"

"Oh, yes," I said. "What is it, Mommy? I want to know if it's treasure."

After another long interval, Mother stood and attempted to dust off her knees. Her hand came away muddy, and she wiped the mud onto the rock outcrop. "I don't know what that is," she said slowly, "I've never seen anything like it. But I would call it treasure."

Happily skipping and jumping, I followed Mother back to the house.

The golden treasure was a slime mold, I later discovered. Since that long-ago morning I have seen a handful of slime molds in damp, unexpected places: one the color of rubies was lurking under a rotten log; another, bright pumpkin-orange, I discovered in the wet cove behind a miniature waterfall; a slime mold of green-yellow that was smooth as an unripe apple I saw clinging to the underside of old wooden stairs; and yet another, rippled gray and silver like moonlit water, was the most recent one I have seen, found under a dense mat of pine needles near a little creek.

Back inside Moms' house that day, I had some milk and Mother had more coffee, and she and Moms talked about buying some material to make dresses. I listened to them contentedly. It had been a good morning. I had set out to find treasure, and I had found treasure. "Life is going to be just like today, always," I thought. It was good to know that I was a finder.

The Spotted Smallmonster

There are things remembered, long gone, that cannot be true. These memories are strange, confusing, and outside the world we know. This is the story of a true memory and a false memory, and how they came together one soft summer evening when the sun went down over the Yankee Fork of the Salmon River.

When I was five, I went fishing with Grandfather Stewart (known to us as *Pa*). It was a cold, blustery day in early June, and anyone with any sense would have had better sense than to go fishing. Pa, however, *went fishing*. That is what he *did*, always.

I was learning to fish, and was thrilled to be asked to go with him. In the Stewart family, fishing was not simply jamming a worm onto a hook and plunking the line into the water. Stewart fishing was grace and art, savvy and synchrony: we were fly fishermen, and we were good. At least, the rest of the Stewarts were good. Dad and Pa had been fly fishing guides, and among their clients were Ernest Hemingway, Nelson Rockefeller, and too many others to name. Locally, they had many admirers, one might even say *worshippers*. Local people would see our Jeep parked at the Trail Creek beaver ponds and would stop merely to watch my dad casting his fly. It was something to see, his line landing straight and true with scarcely a ripple, the fly alighting on the surface of the water just like the pinch of feathers that it was, placed perfectly to get an instant strike from an unwary trout.

At five, I was learning, and even then was doggedly determined to become one of the Stewart fly fishers, well-known in the region for their consummate skill with flies, leader, and the catching of wily trout. On the very first day that Sun Valley resort opened its doors, a lunker of a rainbow trout, eleven pounds plus, caught by Pa in Silver Creek, lay in state in the foyer of Sun Valley Lodge on a bed of ice, showing guests what shining, heavy treasure was to be had for those who hired Sun Valley's guides. Dad was seventeen that day, and guiding was his first adult job.

On this gray June day several years and a World War later, Pa and I jumped into his black 1940 Ford coupe and drove northwest from Ketchum up the road toward Galena Summit. Veering canyon winds bowed the aspens and cottonwoods along Wood River and made the wildflowers bend and sway. It's very difficult to fly fish in strong winds. We both knew this, but nevertheless, we were going fishing.

In a few minutes we had passed North Fork Store and Station, where my little friend Millie lived. After a few more miles, we stopped along Wood River between North Fork Canyon and the bottom of Phantom Hill.

The river was swift and deep there, narrow and savage, with close-spaced trees crowding the banks. On this day the Wood was gravid with high snowmelt, rushing and grinding its way down the valley, opaque and dangerous. This was not a time or a place for a little girl to go fishing. Pa left me to play with streamside pebbles while he walked downstream to see what there was to be seen. As he turned toward the river, I heard Pa mutter, "Looking for places to fish but not today—in July, after high water is done." Ever-present fedora clamped to his head with one hand, he bent into the wind and walked slowly downstream, taking his eyes from the water to wave at me occasionally.

Wood River above North Fork, where the spotted small-monster showed himself to me, an imaginative little girl.

I was cold, but it never occurred to me to get back into the car. After all, we were on a *trip*. We were doing a thing together, sort of, Pa and me.

Although he had lived in Shoshone for many years, now Pa lived in Utah. I seldom saw him, and this was the first time an outing had been just Pa and me. I wasn't a baby anymore; I was a little girl who got to *go*.

I needed a sheltered place to play, and within a few feet of the car, I found a sort of cove, where the river had deposited sand and rounded rocks, backed with a pale-gray jumble of aspen and cottonwood limbs that had been left there during a day when the river was much higher than it was today.

I buttoned my brown wool coat all the way up to the collar and sat in the cove, right at the place where the river rock met a smooth place of coarse sand. A slight depression, the hollow offered some shelter from the wind, and was as fine a place to play as I was likely to find close by. I was a good judge of such places to play, having had a great deal of experience.

With stacked rocks, I decided to make a fairy village of little houses, three rocks for walls and a flat one for each roof, and then I began connecting the houses with tiny paths of sand outlined with pebbles. My head was filled with the loud rushing sound of the river, and I was happy and proud that I was with Pa and that we were on an outing together. His figure got smaller and smaller, but I watched him carefully, and was quick to wave back each time he waved at me.

After a time, I noticed that Pa was getting bigger: he was coming back. This was a good thing, for I had just decided that I was too cold. And besides, I felt funny. I knew that sometimes when I felt funny, it felt like I was being watched by someone or something I could not see. This was how I felt this time.

I felt watched. I got to my feet and dusted sand off my rear with both hands, looking all around in a circle. Nothing was there but me—and Pa—who was back.

"Well," he said, reaching both hands for me and swinging me up to his shoulder, "how's my girl? Let's get in the car and turn on some heat! No fishing for us today. The wind's too strong, and besides, fish can't see flies in cloudy water."

Pa settled me in the front seat on the passenger side of the car and then slid in behind the wheel and turned the key. He reached for the heater knob. A welcome gush of warm air blew right into my face. The car began to back out between the ranks of trees.

But the funny feeling was still there, even though Pa was close and we were safe inside the car. We backed a little more, and a movement outside caught my eye. I turned to look back at my fairy village. Stunned, I saw something long and gray gliding along the ground, just where the little log jam of branches lay across the cobblerock, where I had been sitting only minutes ago.

The thing was mottled gray, silvery as the weathered branches there, and it was as long as I was tall. It looked as big around as my leg and slid smoothly on the rocks. The head had a deep jaw and staring at me though the car window was a large, black-centered eye of vivid yellow.

Was this a snake? No. I knew what snakes were. This creature had a dark-spotted three-inch-high fin starting just behind the eyes and extending halfway down its back like the sail of a dragon or a dinosaur. The fin was translucent like the dorsal fin of a trout, only longer and grayer, and the creature held the fin erect as it looked at me. I was speechless, watching it pour itself away under the tumbled deadwood. In a moment, the thing was gone, and we were gone, too. We were out on the road, heading for home.

"Pa, I saw a monster!" I cried then, feeling as if some paralysis had just been lifted. "It's by the river, back on the rocks!" He pulled over to the edge of the road and stopped.

"A monster?" he asked, dead serious. "What did it look like?"

"It was long and spotted and it was on the ground and . . . " I gasped, running out of breath.

"You must have seen a snake," he said. "But let's go look."

"No," I insisted. "It wasn't a snake. It was a monster, a little one, all spotted, and it had big yellow eyes." I was amazed when Pa turned the coupe around and drove back to the place where we had stopped along the river.

We pulled into our grassy tire tracks once more and Pa got out and searched the small log jam, but no snake was to be seen.

"It must have been a bull snake," he said. "They are spotted. Don't worry, bull snakes can't hurt you."

"Ok," I said. This was Pa, and I didn't want to spoil our first really real outing together. But I knew the thing had not been a snake.

I thought of the thing in capital letters as the Spotted Smallmonster, and eventually I grew to understand that it hadn't been real but must have been an illusion caused by the wind perhaps moving strings of bark on the dead wood. Or by some small creature trundling itself along on the ground near the sticks. Or by the imagination of a small girl immersed in fairy fantasy. Or something.

And yet the memory of the gray, legless creature with the high fin down its back and the staring yellow eye stayed with me and came to me sometimes in dreams, and still does.

But the creature could not have been real. There was no such thing as a Spotted Smallmonster.

****

Twelve years later, I was a Stewart fly fisher, and I was good. I would never be as good as Pa and Dad, but I could hold my own with anyone else. I guided the teenage children of Dad's fly fishing clients and taught them how to cast and how to read the water. I tied my own flies (the Stewart mosquito, of course). I fished every single day that fishing season was open and tried with every cast to be better.

Pa had left us when I was nine, suddenly and irrevocably, a heart attack. I thought of him often as I cast my line and tried to make it land ruler-straight on the water without making the slightest ripple. I hoped Pa would have been proud of me.

My family often camped along the Yankee Fork of the Salmon River, because we had some gold claims there, and also because it was away from the tourist crowd, and was good fishing, if you could cast far enough. We could cast far enough.

Dad was fishing a mile or so from me upstream that warm August afternoon, and I was fishing a good stretch of the Yankee Fork that had some big boulders in the bed that made places for fish to lie behind, though there were no deep holes there. Small willows, bright green grass, and exposed shores of river rock flanked my fishing place, and I stood knee deep in the water, letting the unrelenting chill carry away the heat of late afternoon.

I was casting as far as I could, thinking of the form of each cast, and about making the line lie perfectly each time it landed on the water. "Like feathers," I thought each time the line descended through the air. "Like a length of cobweb stretched tight. Like the faintest breath of air, the lightest touch, the dip of a moth's wing."

With every single cast, I sent out my entire line straight and true, handling the whole length of the thin, braided cord that was attached to my reel, and it felt good. I could cast clear across the Yankee Fork, laying my fly just across the nodding head of a chosen wildflower, and with the tiniest tug, the fly would fall into the water just as if it were a living fly with wings of shining chitin, and not a device I had tied from thread and feathers.

I could not help thinking of something Dad had said earlier that day, however. His words had caught like a fishhook in my mind and would not pull free. We had been eating our picnic sandwiches on a high bank near Preacher's Cove, looking down into clear water and watching a pair of salmon scooping out their nest in the gravel of the creek bed. When the redd was finished, the male twined around the female. We couldn't see them, but we knew that lovely coral-colored eggs were falling into the gravelly nest. In a few weeks, these would hatch into tiny salmon. Nearby and downstream we saw two narrow dark shadows: Dolly Varden trout, waiting and watching for a chance to dine on salmon eggs. This was a sight we saw frequently, fishing as often as we did.

"Take a good look, Danny," Father said thoughtfully. "Remember this day and this pair of salmon, and even the Dollies, because they're all going away. When you are my age, watching salmon digging nests and laying eggs in the Yankee Fork will be a rarity. And then they will go away entirely. I'm sorry that in your lifetime you will see it all disappear. I hope to hell people will realize before they are slipping away forever and will try to bring them back. But I don't think they will."

"But why, Dad?" I asked in dismay. "Everything looks fine to me. The water is clear. There are plenty of insects for the baby fish to eat, and there aren't too many fishermen. What has gone wrong? What's going to happen to the salmon and the Dollies?"

"People are building dams downstream," he said shortly, "and the salmon that spawn here won't be able to get past them. The salmon won't be able to get here when they come back from the sea. And then the Dollies will die, many of them, because they won't have their most important food, and they will go thin into the winters."

"But lots of people love to fish for salmon!" I exclaimed. "No, that won't happen. People won't stand for it. They won't let the salmon go away just for some dams!"

So I stood that afternoon in the sliding cold water casting, and thought of the salmon, how they struggle hundreds of miles from the sea, beat their way up the great Columbia, traverse the Snake, and gain the Salmon River, finally entering the Yankee Fork. They find their places, dig their nests, lay their beautiful translucent eggs, and then, turning gray and lifeless, die in the shallows and lie rotting with their great sunken eyes staring up from the water.

Salmon would never bite my flies, but always slipped past me in the current like phantoms, or rather as if I myself were a phantom, an alien creature not really present in their world. I had watched them many times. I had seen them battering themselves against a new beaver dam until at last the mud-plastered sticks gave way and they could pass. I'd seen them snaking along in water so shallow that their backs were out of water, and I'd seen them, as the light left the water, lying still behind large boulders, taking a few minutes to gather strength for the next run. They swam as if they were coming late to a great event and could not turn aside for any reason. It had always been this way.

I found that I was holding my breath and listening, as if I heard something passing, heard time stretching out long and slipping away from me like the water, and I decided to cross the stream and be away from the place where I now stood. Surely the fishing would be better from the other side.

I had to be very careful in the crossing, for where it is swift and straight, the Yankee Fork is strong and treacherous, with loose slick rock underfoot at every step. I placed my feet with great care, casting my entire line all the while, moving across the smooth-topped river until I stood thigh-deep in the center. The sun, I realized, had nearly set, and the slanting rays showed dancing midges in clouds over the water. The long shadows of lodgepole pine fell across the Yankee Fork from the far bank.

I caught a trout then, and the unexpected pull on the line nearly overbalanced me. I floundered, bending low to keep on my feet. Something cold and smooth caressed my bare leg, and suddenly rising from the water, a great spotted tail lifted until it became a fleshy, translucent veil between my eyes and the setting sun.

Startled, I lurched, lost my fish in a moment of icy terror, and almost fell. The tail slipped beneath the surface, and I suddenly realized that it had been a salmon, and the salmon had gone. My cheek touched the water before I could right myself and I stood for a long moment on one foot, desperately trying not to fall.

Suddenly I felt the cold of the river in my bones, even as I regained my footing. The contact had been electric, and I found that I understood what Dad had meant, every word. Something as ancient and mossy as all time was fading from the world, and soon would be no more. The dams would come and the salmon would go. I knew that now. Father was right. People would not realize what was at stake until it was too late. People would let the salmon go.

I stood and let the water churn around my legs like a pouring of thick glass as I reeled in the long, long line and hooked my fly into the cork grip of the rod. Slowly, I made my way back to the place on the bank from which I had started across the stream. The sun dropped behind the western mountains, and twilight began.

As I put a foot on the bank, I saw cobblerock, a drift of pale sand in a little depression, and a jumble of weathered spindrift.

"The Spotted Smallmonster," I thought, the memory coming to me in a rush.

Suddenly I wondered if the Spotted Smallmonster had been a little girl's nightmare of a dying salmon, a thing flopping about, with gray skinless body, spotted high fins, and sunken pale eyes. But I knew that dying salmon never come in early June. And besides, the Smallmonster had been a *monster*.

I sat on the bank and let it grow dark. As I swatted at invisible mosquitoes and breathed in the cold, sweet scent of wet willow,

QUINNEY

I wondered if I would ever see the Spotted Smallmonster again.

Years have passed, decades, and I have not seen the Spotted Smallmonster whole. But whenever I hear someone tell how the dams have wrought wonders, I seem to see that staring yellow eye.

The Secret of Lily's Garden

My grandmother had a garden, and in her garden was a secret.

In the days when it was legal to dig up wildflowers and plant them at home, my grandmother crafted a wild garden. Her pride and joy was a long border at the south boundary of her lot. Backed by a solid wall of Engelman spruce, a fiery row of Indian paintbrush edged the lawn.

Dug carefully from mountain meadows, her Indian paintbrush bloomed all summer, bringing with it a kind of ragged, vibrant joy no cultivated flower could match. Lily's border was the talk of the neighborhood, and much envied.

The reason for the envy was this: Lily's Indian paintbrush grew and thrived. Others would dig plants of paintbrush, transplant them—and watch them die. Occasionally, such a garden-lover would visit Lily's garden and gaze long at the paintbrush border, wondering.

Two women in particular seemed rather bitter with envy. I thought of them as Miss Tall and Miss Bun. One morning when Lily was gone, I was playing in Lily's garden. The two women strolled by, with long glances at the paintbrush border. "I don't understand it," Miss Tall said to Miss Bun. "My garden has the same soil, the same sun, the same everything. I live only a few blocks away. Lily must have some secret."

"Yes," said Miss Bun. "Let's ask her."

"No!" replied Miss Tall sharply. "We are just as intelligent as

35

My grandparents, Orla and Lily Hicks, in their
garden below the Fourhills.

that woman. To ask would be admitting defeat. Let's watch her. We'll discover her secret."

They never did. But the answer to the riddle was there all along, blooming merrily in the sunshine, in full view of Miss Tall and Miss Bun. Several times I heard my grandmother offer the two ladies "starts" of her paintbrush, adding, "Would you like to know my secret for growing them?" She had told me the secret a year before the two ladies began coming to look at her garden.

Once, Miss Bun took home some of the offered "starts." Every day for two weeks I checked her garden from a watching place inside a lilac bush on the corner of the next-door property; the paintbrush starts withered and died. The two ladies would always say, "No, Lily, we can see perfectly well how you grow them," and refuse the eager-to-be-shared knowledge of the secret.

At five, I knew. I knew what Lily had discovered by patient observation in the wild meadows where she had found her original plants. Now, after so many years, my own Indian paintbrush plants, started from seed gathered in the wild, raise exuberant shaggy heads to the sun on our hill. I won't wait for you to ask.

Here is Lily's secret: Indian paintbrush is a parasite. To survive, the roots of paintbrush must attach to the roots of some other perennial plant, preferably a shrub. Without this support, paintbrush will die. Lily dug her first Indian paintbrush from wet meadows in the Pioneer Mountains, and her stubby fingers felt among the roots as she lifted the plants from the soil. After several trials with plants that died, she dug more, washed dirt from their roots, and turned with her shovel to the shrubs nearby.

In Lily's garden, standing just behind the flaming row of paintbrush, bloomed a line of shrubby cinquefoil, bright with buttercup-yellow flowers. Below the surface of the soil, intertwined roots told the story. Lily showed me the secret when I was four, and I have never forgotten.

We are such visual beings now, bombarded by images of all sorts every hour of our waking lives. We often think that appearance is all; more dangerously, we believe we have instant, complete understanding merely from seeing. Many times, Lily told me, *Watch. Wait. Ask. Learn.*

Dust

From the perspective of the years, certain memories come back to me whole, shining, and clear as if they happened yesterday and I am still a schoolgirl in ribbon-tied braids.

I was in the first grade, six years old, and had been a schoolgirl for all of two weeks. Like the other girls in my class, I loved school, and like them I loved playing hide and seek, jacks, and especially hopscotch, at recess time. Our school had almost the only sidewalks in town, so even after school we would play hopscotch at school, close by our first-grade classroom windows.

Across a dirt street from our hopscotch-sidewalk were several houses where families lived. But one of the houses was different. Behind close-set lilac bushes, its yard was weedy and dry, enclosed by a gap-toothed picket fence. No one had watered the lawn and trees for a long time. No one had painted either the fence or its house in years. Dingy white paint was peeling and flaking into the brittle grass, giving way to gray weathered wood.

The house looked sad without a family, I thought. I walked past the empty house every day on the way to and from school and often wondered why it was empty and what had happened to its people.

One day I noticed a broken window. On another day, some big boys pulled a few pickets from the fence and used them for sword fighting.

After several frosty nights, the silver poplars in the old house's yard turned to gold. The unwatered grass, parched to yellow, didn't look so bad now that everything was dying back with the autumn. The old house looked friendlier now. Sometimes I would stop at the fence and hold two pickets in my hands while I peered through the lilac bushes at the old house, wondering.

One day after school my friend Donna and I were the last ones remaining after a game of hopscotch. It had been a brilliant blue day, and the sun was sinking in the west toward the Warm Springs hills. There was little daylight left, and we knew it. A chilly wind came up; sunset at 6,000 feet can be cold in September. We stood side by side on the sidewalk for some time looking at the hopscotch squares, wondering whether we should start another game, unwilling to go home. "I know!" I said. "Nobody is around. Let's go inside the old house!"

We crossed the crisp lawn and went right up to the door. All was silent.

This was a forbidden thing.

No one had ever told us to keep away from the old house, but this is the kind of thing you know when you are a little girl. This was different from sneaking an extra cookie or looking at books under the covers with a flashlight when you were supposed to be asleep, or not hanging up your coat. Going into a strange house was really quite a bad thing, when you weren't invited. I saw my hand on the starry glass doorknob, and the knob turned. We went in.

The first room was shadowy and cool. I remember pale wallpaper, and on the floor, linoleum worn to the black backing in the centers of the doorways. And I remember dust.

The next room was the kitchen. A wood stove still stood there, a squat green and tan Depression-era stove with the water-bath bin and wood box, one like Tommy's grandma had. Pale squares on the wallpaper showed where pictures had been taken away.

We stepped through a doorway into a room where we could see sunlight. This was a bedroom on the west side, light falling into the room through a large sash window. It was quite a large room, with a dirty wooden floor. In the room, I remember four things: an iron bedstead with ugly bare springs; a tall oval mirror in a frame-stand on the floor; a broken chair overturned in the center of the room—and next to one wall, a big wooden trunk.

We ran right to the trunk and opened it.

Wonders spilled out: feather boas and an ostrich-feather fan. A smooth dove-grey hat with a face veil and white quill plumes. A silvery flapper d ress w ith s paghetti s traps and bugle beads hanging in strings of fringe from the hem. A black lace shawl, sewn with sequins in many colors. A pair of high-heeled shoes with chunky heels, each shoe sporting a great bow of black faille centered with a cluster of rhinestones. Two real muskrat skins sewn together, complete with glass eyes, leather noses, and little legs and tails, a clamp in the mouth of each so they could be fastened around a woman's shoulders as a stole. A small doll wearing a rose-sprigged nightgown.

I picked up the doll and examined her closely, because I had never seen a doll like her. She had a stuffed cotton body, but her head-with-neck-and-upper-chest, and arms and legs, were made of porcelain. A cap of wavy hair was molded into her head, and she had painted features—blue eyes, delicate cupid's-bow lips, and threadlike eyebrows. Black shoes and white stockings had been painted right onto her porcelain legs and feet.

I put the little doll aside and pulled out a full, swirling skirt of green plaid taffeta. Donna found a long-sleeved satin blouse with a deep v-neck and covered buttons all down the back, in glossy midnight blue.

But there were other wonders: a black wool gown, slim and straight, its puffed sleeves sparkling with jet beads. A white housedress with a square neck and a sash that tied in the back,

41

printed all over with tiny blue and orange flowers. Slip-on mules with draggly marabou feathers. A length of wide pink ribbon. A coat of plush black mouton with deep cuffs and huge celluloid buttons. A straw hat with red velvet roses. A purple turban, arranged in intricate pleats, with a veil of the same color. A man's brown tweed sport jacket. There were more, but these are all I remember.

We pulled things from the trunk and tried them on, and as the light slanted lower through the window, we began to play in front of the mirror. The glass was blotchy and dark in places and sported a nest of cracks near the top, as if someone had thrown a bottle at it in a fit of anger, but we didn't care.

Donna pranced back and forth in the mules with a feather boa dashingly draped around her neck and the sequined shawl tied over her school blouse. I chose the meltingly soft mouton coat and the dove-grey hat with its pale veil and white quills.

We were going to the opening night of a Hollywood movie. We were starlets on our way to nightclubs in New York City. We were brides ready to leave on a honeymoon cruise to Rio. We were rich society ladies invited to dinner with the President and First Lady at the White House.

We whirled and twirled in the wide bar of sunlight falling through the window. I can see us at this moment, the dust from the floor rising and spinning around us in shining motes like little stars.

A fairy time, some dusting of magic from a far place, was given to two little girls, a sprinkling of dreams reflected dimly in a dirty mirror. A day out of time, at once from the past: the clothing—and from the future: the young women we would grow to be. We were beautiful.

But all too soon the tiny stars went out one by one as the sun slipped away and sank behind the far hills. Donna and I curtsied as we were introduced to the First Lady—and found ourselves standing on a gritty floor in a strange old house, eerily reflected in a crazy mirror.

We remembered to be cold, and suddenly were pierced by the knowledge that we were late—very late—in coming home from school. Our parents would be looking for us. We had done what we should not do.

Being sensible little girls, we hurriedly stuffed the finery into the trunk and shut it with care. We knew about mice.

Donna and I parted at the corner, and I ran all the way home. Three blocks can seem like a mile in the cold twilight when you have done the wrong thing.

But at home, no one had noticed that I had not come directly from school, a very strange thing in itself. Relieved, I sat down to dinner with Mom and Daddy. My little sister Vicki, only a few days old, had already been put to bed in her crib. Perhaps because a new baby had upset the household routine, I had escaped being questioned about why I had been late.

I hugged to myself the secret in the old house. Donna and I had promised each other that we would go back the next day right after school, as soon as the other girls went home. We had not seen everything in the trunk!

I drifted to sleep that night imagining things we might find in the trunk the next day. After all, if you were packing, wouldn't you pack your best stuff first? So the things on the bottom might be ball gowns or skating costumes like the one Mom wore when she skated in the ice shows, or even mink coats or diamond necklaces.

Anything could be waiting in the trunk, anything at all.

I floated through the school day in anticipation and joined Donna and the other girls at the hopscotch sidewalk as soon as we were let out for the day. After what seemed a long time, the hopscotch party began to lose interest. "One more game," said the leader. I stepped close to Donna. "Oh, boy," I whispered. "As soon as they're gone, we can go to the old house." I loved sharing an important secret.

"What old house?" Donna said, much too loudly. "What are you talking about?" The other girls stared at me.

"Why, the old house we went to yesterday," I said, not wanting to point at the house. The gray roof was quite visible from the sidewalk. "Remember what we found?"

"No," Donna said firmly. "I don't know what you mean." Her expression was as cold as her voice.

The secret burst out of me. "Don't you remember the trunk with the beautiful dress-up clothes, Donna?"

"I don't remember any trunk and I don't remember any dress-up clothes." She turned away and picked up her hop-scotch marker.

On the edge of the group of little girls, I stood on the sidewalk alone, in a world different from theirs, bright and strange. Was this the first time I knew that I was not like them? I felt a chill and ghostly finger on the back of my neck. A shadow touched me then, and it has never left me.

I didn't return to the old house that day, but walked home very slowly, and for the first time that I remember, thought about what was real and what was pretend, and how they were different.

A few days later I did go back to the old house.

The glass knob on the front door turned just as easily. Inside, it was colder. The heavy stove still hunched against the kitchen wall.

In the bedroom, the discolored mirror reflected my green-and-white gingham school dress. The old chair still lay upside down in the middle of the floor, and the iron bedstead stood where it had been before. But the trunk was gone. Or had there ever been a trunk full of treasures in this dirty room?

I stood motionless, shocked. The sunlight streamed through the window and showed me a white gleam on the floor near the wall.

I bent and held in my hand a small porcelain doll's leg with painted shoe and stocking.

Hollyhock Dolls

Mother was having coffee with two neighbor women one sunny summer morning. I was seven, busy in the living room playing with my small plastic horses. From the kitchen came the delicious, almost overpowering perfume of hot cinnamon rolls.

"I don't care," Mrs. Wilson was saying. "I come right out and tell my two girls to stay away from Bea Cameron's house. That woman—well, she hates children. You know how she is. She might be dangerous."

"You may be right, Grace," said Mrs. White, tut-tutting. "You may well be right."

My mother said nothing.

"Well, Bernice?" Mrs. Wilson said after a time of silence that had stretched too long. "Aren't you worried about that woman and your own girls? After all, the Cameron house is less than three blocks from your front door. Danny must walk that way to and from school."

"I hadn't thought about it," Mother said.

"It's time you did," said Mrs. White.

I could hear Mother pouring coffee, but she did not reply.

I gathered my plastic horses and put them into their box in the bottom shelf of the bookcase. "Mom?" I called. "I'm going to walk down to the school and play on the swings for a while."

Mother came into the doorway cradling her coffee, both hands folded around her cup as if it were a wounded bird. "All

45

right, Danny," she said. "Be home by lunchtime."

"I will." I skipped out the door and down the hill on the nameless dirt road that was our street. At the corner I turned and went another way from my usual straight-two-blocks route. Like all children I was curious, and I wondered what there could be about Mrs. Cameron that made the other mothers dislike her.

Mr. and Mrs. Cameron had no children. They lived in a very small log cabin behind the Jack Frost Motel, less than a block from Ketchum Grade School. The cabin was situated so close to the rear of the motel that there was no room for a lawn, and precious little room for anything at all. The cabin fronted no street. The only way to get there was from a dirt alleyway, dusty and weedy.

I walked past the motel and peered down the alley. I saw no one, so I walked a little way toward the cabin.

Unpainted and with cement chinking between the logs, the cabin had been there since just about forever. The small-paned windows of the front room faced the windowless back wall of the Jack Frost Motel. From the cabin, the beautiful golden sweep of the slopes of Dollar Mountain could not be seen at all, only a small triangle that was Dollar's very top. A thin slice of beaten dirt gave way to a wooden stoop and above that, to a narrow door painted dark green.

But along the front of the cabin, someone had planted a row of hollyhocks. The hollyhocks were in full flower, blooming in every color of the red-pink-white-yellow-apricot family, and the flowers were busy with bumblebees. To me, the hollyhocks looked irresistibly appealing. I was a child who loved flowers, and we didn't have hollyhocks at our house.

Still, no one was to be seen, and as if operating on their own, my tennis shoes began to take me closer and closer to the tall hollyhocks, so close that I could hear the bumbling whir of the bees' dark wings. I reached out a hand to one of the flowers.

46

Suddenly the green door opened. I pulled in my hand and took an involuntary step back.

Standing on the step was a short, grim-faced woman with hair smoothly gathered into two long, black braids. I knew who she must be and took another step backward. "Hello, Mrs. Cameron," I said shakily. "I was just looking at your flowers."

She stood silent for a moment, feet set apart on the wooden boards of the step. She stared at me so intently that I felt that her eyes would bore right through me. She said abruptly, "Have you ever made hollyhock dolls?"

"No," I began, more than ready to leave, "but I have to—"

Mrs. Cameron cut me off. "We're going to make them. I'll teach you." Suddenly she had my hand. Her own hand was hard and strong and dry. "Come inside while I put the kettle on," she said. "We'll have tea after a bit."

I pulled back just a little and she let go my hand, but something in her face changed, and I, a shy child who did not like to be touched, took the hand that had fallen away. We went through the green door.

Inside, the house was clean and neat, with a small table and a shelf on the wall holding a row of fancy teacups and their matching saucers. I sat at the table while Mrs. Cameron put the kettle on to boil.

She indicated the teacups. "Which one do you want for your tea?" she asked. I pointed at one painted with lovely copper-colored roses. Mrs. Cameron chose one with pink daisies. She set the cups with their delicate saucers on the table and said, "The kettle will sing when it's time." She took a small box of toothpicks from the kitchen counter and put it into the pocket of her skirt.

We went back outside to the hollyhocks.

I felt awkward at first, But Mrs. Cameron, full skirt and all, sat right down in the dirt. "I'll make my doll first," she said, "and then I'll help you do one."

She plucked a pink flower and snapped off the stalk, leaving a short length of stem attached to the flower. Then she chose a bud of the same color, a small, tight bud. Deftly, she stripped away the green sepals from the bottom of the fat bud. "Look at these little holes here," she told me.

"Why, those are eyes," I exclaimed.

Mrs. Cameron smiled for the first time. With her thumbnail, she nipped off the pointed top of the "head," and stuck the bud onto the stalk-end of the upended flower, fastening them together with a toothpick. "Look," she said, her eyes sparkling. "She's a lady."

"Oh!" I said, mesmerized. "Oh, do let me make one!" I chose a peach-colored blossom and bud, and with a little help, soon I had my own doll.

"These ladies are going to a ball at the palace, and they aren't finished dressing," Mrs. Cameron said. "My lady has to put on her bonnet." She picked another pink flower and pulled off two adjacent petals. Breaking a toothpick in two, she attached the "bonnet" to the head of her doll. The effect was magical, with the tiny eyes peering from the smooth face under the shade of a ruffle-edged bonnet that would have done a Victorian lady proud. I made a peach-colored bonnet for my own doll. Then the teakettle sang and we took our dolls in for tea.

Sipping tea from the rose-painted cup, I faced Mrs. Cameron across the table. At the same time, I felt both grown up and very small. After all, grown women took tea from fine cups and held their little fingers out to the side, just so, as we were doing. But it was also true that small girls had tea parties with their dolls and talked about castles and clouds and gowns and dreams, as we were doing. Our dolls matched our cups and sat right in the middle of the tablecloth, watching.

Over tea, I learned from Mrs. Cameron that a lady arriving at a ball would look at once for a handsome prince to dance with her. This was the way it was done.

We went back out into the sunshine.

From long, large buds that were unopened, plus small buds for heads, we made princes and gave them matching cloaks as well.

We made more ladies and more princes. Mrs. Cameron fashioned an especially grand prince from buds of deep maroon. I surprised myself by choosing white and making a bride with a veil.

And then the dolls danced, two by two, while the others leaned against the bottom of the step waiting their turns. We sang to make music for the dancing, and we whirled the dolls in the sunlight, back and forth, up and down, as if, like fairies, they could fly.

Through our voices, I was hearing something else. I stopped singing. "Danny, Daannneeee." It was Mother, calling me home to lunch. I had not thought of time.

Mrs. Cameron stopped singing, too. "I guess you have to go now," she said, getting to her feet and shaking dust from her skirt. She sounded different, formal.

"Yes," I said. "I promised Mom I would be back at lunchtime. May I take my peach doll home?"

"Of course," Mrs. Cameron said. "and her prince."

I remembered my manners. "Thank you," I said, feeling rather strange once more. Then the strangeness melted away and I spun around in the dust of the alley. 'Oh, Mrs. Cameron, I had fun! Did you have fun? I love making hollyhock dolls and having tea, don't you? I will never forget how to make them and I will show all my friends. Can I come back and see you? Can we have tea and make more dolls?

She said, "Yes, Danny, come back tomorrow. Be sure to come back tomorrow. And you can have all the hollyhocks you want, even if I don't come to the door." There was a pause. "I don't always come to the door," she finished.

"Thank you, Mrs. Cameron! Goodbye!" I sped down the

alley, wings on my feet. When I reached the street I looked back to wave, but she had gone inside.

I ran almost all the way home.

Eagerly I showed Mother my two peach-colored dolls and showed her their tiny eyes and how the bonnet went on, and how you could make a prince using a long, pointed bud. I was proud of my lady and her prince.

"They are very pretty, Danny," Mom said, then added, "Bea Cameron taught you?"

"Yes," I said, and told her how we had tea from the fine painted cups and how we sang and danced the dolls all around.

"Bea Cameron," Mother said as if to herself. "Tomorrow we will go see her and thank her together," she said. "I haven't talked to Bea for . . ." She broke off in mid-sentence and said no more.

"Do we have a teacup that would match my dolls?" I asked Mom. After looking through the cupboards, at last she handed me a small juice glass with oranges and orange blossoms printed on clear glass.

"I guess this is the closest match," she said. So we leaned the peach-colored lady and the peach-colored prince against the orange-printed orange-juice glass, one on either side, in the middle of the kitchen table.

The next morning halfway to lunchtime, Mother and I walked down the hill to Mrs. Cameron's cabin. Bold and upright, this morning the hollyhock forest had damp feet. Someone had watered the row not long before. Mother knocked on the green door.

No one came to the door.

"Mrs. Cameron said that she doesn't always come to the door," I offered. "She said I could pick hollyhock flowers and make dolls anytime I want." But somehow, I knew it wouldn't the same without Mrs. Cameron.

Mother looked at the door for what seemed like a long time.

We trudged back up the hill, and that was that. Mother returned to her housework and I went to find Carol and Joyce to play horses.

The next morning I went back to Mrs. Cameron's, but she didn't come to the door. And I came again the next morning, and the next, but I didn't see her.

I never saw Mrs. Cameron at all.

Eventually I realized that the hollyhock plants were parched and wilting, so I asked the closest neighbor, Mrs. Brohan, if I could use her hose to water them.

Every time I came from then on, Mrs. Brohan would call out, "Here to water your hollyhocks, Danny?" I loved those hollyhocks and showed some of my girlfriends how to make the dolls, but I knew the hollyhocks were not mine.

I watered the hollyhocks several times a week all summer, but I never saw Mrs. Cameron. I wondered if she were inside the cabin behind the curtains, sipping tea from the daisy-painted teacup, watching me. I wondered if I had done something wrong.

I never saw Mrs. Cameron again. Years later I learned that Bea Cameron had gone or had been taken to the Idaho State Mental Hospital at Blackfoot, as nearly as I can figure, on the day after we had made the dolls.

To this day, I don't know why, and I don't know what happened to her in the end—if she was released eventually, or if she remained in the asylum for the rest of her life. Mr. Cameron eventually married another woman, and, oddly, she and I became fast friends despite the gap in our ages. But I never made hollyhock dolls with the new Mrs. Cameron.

Dollar Mountain still slopes down and down to clear Trail Creek and its dark-green borders of aspen and cottonwood. My old street is paved now; you would know it as Spruce Street. The small cabin still squats in the same dusty alley, behind a line of adjoining shops that once made up the Jack Frost Motel.

QUINNEY

And the hollyhocks there grow only in my memory.

The View from Stewart Granger's Snowshoes

Stewart Granger starred in innumerable films in a career that spanned fifty years, from the early 1930s to the 1970s. These include, among many others, *Scaramouche, King Solomon's Mines, Young Bess, Bhowani Junction, All the Brothers Were Valiant, Moonfleet, The Dance of the Seven Veils, Sodom and Gomorrah, The Last Hunt, Footsteps in the Fog, Prisoner of Zenda, Harry Black and the Tiger, Beau Brummell*, and a movie I know well, *The Wild North*, which was released in 1952.

It is difficult to believe that not everyone knows of this sophisticated, dashing, handsome, athletic, and refined gentleman actor. If you do not, dive into a Stewart Granger film!

In addition to his regular job, during the 1950s and 1960s my father, Clayton Stewart, was the Idaho "contact man" for the film giant Metro-Goldwyn-Meyer. During that time, MGM shot portions of a number of films in central Idaho. The director, stars, and technical crew would stay at Sun Valley resort. My father worked for Sun Valley, and it was definitely in the resort's interest to keep MGM's people happy. For many years, Dad had been a hunting and fishing guide as well as an avid outdoorsman, and he knew the mountain canyon country intimately, so he was a logical choice for contact man.

It was Dad's job to listen to the director's needs and find places that would work for the scripts: "I need a river with a grove of tall trees near the bank and a small hill sloping down

Looking toward Dollar Mountain and Sun Valley Road
from our yard.

to the grove," the director said he needed for *The Tall Men*. "I need an avalanche that we can film safely." That became a scene in *Seven Brides for Seven Brothers*. "I need an isolated gas station with snowy mountains behind and snow all around it"— and Dad recommended North Fork Store and Station for the Marilyn Monroe movie *Bus Stop*. These were the kinds of places Dad would find for the MGM directors.

In 1950, MGM was filming *The Wild North*, a "snowy western" about a fugitive fur trapper (Stewart Granger) and the relentless lawman (Wendell Corey) who pursues him, with Cyd Charisse as the love interest. Dad suggested the Boulder Mountains northwest of Ketchum as a good backdrop for the outdoor shooting. Sun Valley had sled dog teams then, and these were called into service.

Filming those scenes from the *The Wild North* was complex. Equipment broke or ground to a halt in the subzero midwinter cold at 7,000 feet. The dog teams had to be wrangled, people and camera equipment had to be kept warm, the midday meal had to be transported and served, and most importantly— snow is a MOST unforgiving medium.

A film crew and setup personal can leave no tracks in a snow scene. If snow is tracked in a first attempt at filming a scene and the scene needs to be re-shot, the location is ruined as a pristine place where no action has supposedly taken place before, and the entire scene must be moved elsewhere for the next take.

In this film, the actors wore snowshoes in many of the scenes—not the small, round "bear-paw" type, but real, honest-to-goodness trapper-type snowshoes made from bent wood and lacquered rawhide. These were nearly five feet long and very narrow, with sharply upcurved tips and rawhide ties to attach to one's boots. It takes some doing to manage these. Stewart Granger, I must say, mastered them.

I was a little girl of seven when *The Wild North* was being filmed, a little girl who hated winter.

Every winter the snow was deep, and there was nowhere for a little girl to be alone outdoors. There was nowhere for a little girl to go except the beginners' ski mountain, the skating rink, and the plowed roads and driveways. I would try to get to my beloved Fourhills and fields, but with the snow as deep as my head was high, I could never get more than a few dozen yards off a plowed road without becoming utterly exhausted.

One day my mother took me up to the Sun Valley garage to meet Dad at the end of a day of filming of *The Wild North*.

It must have been the last—or nearly the last—day of filming, and I must have looked rather appealing, because Stewart Granger gave me his snowshoes. "Here, little Stewart," he said, kneeling so that his eyes looked straight into mine, "I present you with these snowshoes from another Stewart." The only other thing I remember about the encounter is that I was speechless, and that he had very white teeth and smiling eyes that seemed very bright and intelligent indeed.

We took the snowshoes home.

Laboriously, I tied my red rubber boots into the new snowshoes. I took one step and fell right onto my face in the driveway. I was not expecting this!

My mother explained to me that they were men's snowshoes, and they were much too large for me. But they were *mine*, and I was not about to give them up.

The next day I tried again, and again, and *again* to walk in the snowshoes, which were longer than I was tall! It took me several weeks before I could use the snowshoes to walk anywhere but on a packed-snow driveway, but I would not give up.

Eventually I did learn to use them well, and then the world of winter opened wide. No longer was I limited to a very small distance from plowed roads. No longer was Dollar Mountain, with its noisy crowds of skiers, the only place a very small girl like me could get away from houses and roads during the months of deep snow. In the summer I could walk away from the house and at once be alone in the fields and hills. Now I could do the same in winter.

Hardly anyone snowshoed in Ketchum and Sun Valley when I was a child. I was the only snowshoer I ever saw, for more than ten years. Snowmobiles were a thing yet to come, and there were very few cross-country skiers and virtually no back-country skiers, so all the unplowed, un-skied places were untracked, untouched, unpeopled.

I fell often every time I attempted a slope, but I kept on and gained a world of wonders. After a subzero night, the surface of the snow, where untrampled, transformed into a world of rainbow diamonds every moment that the sun or moon shone in the sky. Shadows of trees became long, blue spiders as the sun moved westward toward Adam's Gulch. I found tiny trails left by mice and voles, and deep tracks left by deer and elk. I saw snow midges, tiny flies with iridescent wings and fuzzy antennae, hovering over the snow and walking through the miniature forests of ice crystals on the surface. I discovered secret hollows in trees where mosses, as green as they would be in spring, hid from the sharp winds. Atop four feet of snow, I was tall, and I could look into last year's bird nests in the familiar aspens along Trail Creek.

Winter was no longer a prison. I was now part of winter, just as I had always been part of fall, spring and summer.

I lived on those snowshoes every winter until I went to college. I studied on snowshoes, I picnicked on snowshoes, I wrote stories and songs on snowshoes, I learned to use my Brownie Starflash camera on snowshoes, I came close to foxes and deer and voles and elk and sage grouse and coyotes and—snowshoe rabbits, of course—while on snowshoes. I saw the sun and moon rise and set, and I dreamed on snowshoes for years, until the rawhide ties at last wore out.

QUINNEY

Then Mom cleaned my snowshoes for the last time and hung them on the stone wall of our sunroom, crossed trophies from 1950, my doors into winter.

Thank you, Stewart Granger.

Just a Story of Murder

As a child, I was a *watcher*. Yes, I was a doer, and yes, I was a dreamer, but at all times I was a watcher, and am a watcher still. When you set yourself to watch, you will see things. It's rather like being a finder, a finder of the insubstantial.

I was seven years old, a sturdy little girl with straight bangs and flyaway butterscotch hair. The hills and fields near home were where I lived. I knew all the dogs, all the horses, all the wildflowers, all the rock outcrops, and some of the people in my neighborhood. I began to think in stories, and told stories about gnomes and demons, fairies and elves, birds that talked and little girls who could fly. Some of the stories were real, and some were not. My family was sometimes at a loss as to whether I was describing true events or whether I was telling one of my stories. I knew the difference.

I liked to lie behind a small rock outcrop near the Ketchum-Sun Valley Road and watch what traffic came past. Between our house and the rock outcrop was an alfalfa field owned by Sun Valley Resort, a field that grew hay for the horses who worked at Sun Valley Stables. To get to this watching place, all I had to do was run out the door, trot across a corral, and follow an irrigation ditch through the alfalfa field to the rock place near Sun Valley Road.

The rock outcrop could not be farmed, an unproductive blemish on the land at the eastern edge of the field. It was a good watching place. Next to the road, a pole fence bounded the field. Across the road, there was a dusty footpath and an identical fence, and the land then fell away very sharply toward Trail Creek in a slippery fifty-foot slide of cobbles, dirt, and gravel. Two hundred feet to the north stood a long and narrow red-painted hay barn owned by Sun Valley. Across from my watching place, another barn stood, a large and unpainted barn, crazily perched right at the edge of the slope down to the creek.

It was a bright, hot morning in early June. Reveling in the fact that school was out for the summer, I settled into my usual place in the dust and began to watch.

There were walkers, runners, people on horseback, a car or two every five or ten minutes, dogs going about dog business, and small things doing their small living: butterflies, birds, bees, caterpillars, mice, ants. Concealed behind the rocks, I could watch them all.

The harvester ants here were a strangeness in the landscape, the only colonies of their kind I had found in my world. (I was later to find them common in the low desert eighty miles south.) When the rodeo was on, the Indian performers camped at the rock outcrop. I always searched the anthills for tiny bits of real turquoise among the neat mounds of same-sized pebbles the ants piled around their homes, and once in a while I would find one, a great prize for a small girl.

One slender woman ran past every morning, often dressed all in white, running with a kind of clean grace that was hers alone. I knew this was Norma Shearer, the celebrated actress, who had forsaken the silver screen for a more private existence. I saw limousines coming from the Ketchum railroad depot, bringing Very Important People for a stay at Sun Valley. Daddy let me look into the limousines when they were parked in the Sun Valley garage, and I knew that each one had two cut-glass vases attached to its walls in the back seat, to hold fresh flowers. I knew that the big gray-muzzled black Labrador loping along the path was named Boy, and that he was going downtown to hang around Hegstrom's Drug Store, to see if anyone would toss him something good to eat—some saltines, maybe, or a few potato chips. The fiery sorrel gelding trotting by was a friend: Flake his name was, and his rider, Mike, kept his hide polished to mirror-brightness. I knew many people by name, but I never revealed myself to them. The rock outcrop was, after all, a watching place.

The morning was growing old, and soon I would have to go; it was nearly lunchtime. Mother would make for us bologna and lettuce sandwiches on soft bread, neatly cut in half and flanked by piles of potato chips, with full glasses of milk as well. On a lucky day, there might be sliced peaches or Jell-O. I got to my knees, ready to go, and almost, almost stood up. But then I heard the shouting.

Two men were shouting, and they were inside the old barn. The barn had no insulation, I knew—shafts and polka-dots of sunlight came right through the roof and walls when I had looked in the door weeks before.

I couldn't understand what words they were saying, save one word only, "You." They shouted angrily, and every once in a while I understood the word "you," but that was all. A robin sitting on the apex of the barn roof flew off, rollercoastering over my head. The men's anger filled the air and rooted me in my watching place. I had never heard men shouting like that before. It sounded dangerous.

After a short time, a man strode from the old barn, heading for the hay barn further north down the footpath. I remember him well, except for his face: he was tall (but don't all men seem tall to a seven-year-old child?). He had dark hair and wore a white long-sleeved shirt. The man looked at the ground, hands shoved hard into the pockets of his jeans. With his long strides, it took him no time at all to disappear into the black, shadowed mouth of the red hay barn.

I hesitated. Should I go home? Lunch was calling, and besides, I felt very uncomfortable now. But I stayed still, like a rabbit in a bush watching coyotes go by.

Suddenly the man in the white shirt burst from the shadowed doorway of the hay barn. The second man, a smaller man, I saw for the first time. He came out from the unpainted barn and stood still in the late-morning sunshine, watching the other man come toward him. It was odd, I thought, that this man was standing on the inside of the fence, right at the top of the rocky slide down to the creek, instead of on the path outside the fence, where everyone else walked.

"That's funny," I remember thinking. "Why doesn't he walk outside the fence, on the path?"

The next part I have played over in my mind so often that it is like a worn tape gone fuzzy with slow-motion drag. Though I cannot remember what he wore or what he looked like, I see him. The smaller man flung out both arms, holding them like wings jutting from his shoulders, as if he were about to fly. Then I saw the rifle.

The man in the white shirt put the stock up to his shoulder and laid his cheek down like I had seen Daddy do so many times when he was target shooting. In my memory I can hear the bolt sliding and clicking home, though I don't know if that is a true part of what I could then perceive. I do know that the rifle was bolt-action, because there was a rifle just like it in the gun cabinet in my parents' bedroom, and I had seen Daddy oil it and work the bolt.

The smaller man began to run back toward the old barn. The man in the white shirt looked up and down the road, both ways. No cars were coming. He fired the rifle, and the sound came to me at once: a flat *snap*. The smaller man pitched forward and disappeared.

I blinked. This couldn't have happened. Grown-ups don't

just come out of barns and shoot each other. This could not have happened.

But then I heard it: a sound I understood, because I had slid down that steep, gravelly slope many times, shoes swallowed up in dirt and rocks. Something heavy was sliding, sliding and rolling, gathering momentum and rolling faster and faster down the slope to the river. "That man was shot," I thought. "He is not just crouching down below the edge of the slope and hiding. He is rolling down to the creek, too fast. I know that a person running down the slope cannot get down it that fast." The sound stopped abruptly.

Transfixed, I watched the man in the white shirt carry the rifle back into the hay barn. I waited a long, long time, but he did not come out.

Slowly I wormed my way back from the rock outcrop, until I was well back in the alfalfa. Getting to my feet then, I ran. I ran all the way back to the house.

"Mommy, Mommy, a man shot another man down by Trail Creek!" I shouted as I pulled open our front door.

"Sit down at the table and drink some milk, Danny," my mother said calmly. She wiped her hands on a dishtowel and sat at the table beside me. Between bites of sandwich and potato chips, I told her the whole story. "Come on," I said, very excited. "Let's call the marshal. Let's go with him to see if the shot man is still alive."

"Don't worry about him," Mother said, shaking more potato chips onto my plate. "I'm sure he is all right. And don't worry about the man with the rifle. He was probably just looking down the sights for fun, and the other man went back into the barn. Grown-ups don't just come out of barns and shoot each other." She patted my shoulder and left the room.

I sat for a long time looking at my empty glass and crumb-strewn plate. "She thinks this is a story," I thought. And there was nothing I could think of to do—except one thing only, and that would have to wait.

The next morning when the sun came up I stood at the top of the gravelly slope and looked down to the creek where the body should have been. Someone had been down or up the slope recently. There were big, vague tracks everywhere, indented deeply and anonymously into the soft, cobbly gravel of the slope.

But, after all, there were horses inside that fence. And people, including me, went down to Trail Creek all the time to go fishing. Children slid down the slope to go inner-tubing in the creek. Anyone could have made those tracks. I stood at the top of the slope for a long time, but the ground had nothing more to tell me.

The alfalfa field is now gone, and Our Lady of the Snows Catholic Church stands in the place where the rodeo Indians once camped. My rock outcrop blends into the church's lawn and flowerbeds like a clever and extremely expensive bit of landscaping. The pole fence, many times repaired, still remains, as does the long hay barn. The older barn has gone. The paths on both sides of Sun Valley Road are now blacktopped, maintained and very busy. The road itself hums with traffic night and day.

Mother was right. Many years have now gone, and my little-girl tale is only a story. The gravelly slope has seen many tracks of many kinds, I am sure, and Trail Creek keeps its secrets.

Mom (in the middle of the second seat in the surrey)
at the Sun Valley Rodeo.

Crusader Turtle

His suit of armor was formed of steel, richly inlaid with gold, and the device on his shield was of a young oak tree pulled up by the roots, with the Spanish word Desdichado, *signifying* Disinherited.

—*Sir Walter Scott, Ivanhoe*

I was eight years old, and even at that tender age, I knew the credo of shoppers who lived in Ketchum, Idaho. This pearl of shopping wisdom was simply this: "You can get it in Twin." In the 1950s, you could buy groceries, gasoline, cigarettes, film, pencils, comic books, aspirin, and post cards in Ketchum. But shoes, clothing, books, furniture, tools, fabric, automobiles, and everything else, you had to get in Twin Falls, a modest city 85 miles to the south on Highway 93. School clothes and school shoes came from Twin; the family car came from Twin; the dentist was in Twin; toys were in Twin.

And so were goldfish and baby turtles, in two large tanks at the Woolworth's store there. Baby turtles were fifty cents. For an additional dollar-twenty-five you could add a round plastic bowl with a little ramp from the water to a tiny island, from which sprouted a bright green and fragile plastic palm tree. And for a quarter more, you could buy a metal can marked "Turtle Food: Select Ant Eggs."

At Woolworth's, Mother went for things like safety pins

and needles, notebooks for school, scarves and mittens, nylon stockings, can openers, scissors. I went straight to the pet department and examined with passionate interest the canaries and parakeets, the goldfish and turtles.

For some time, Mom would not let me have a turtle. "They are cute, Danny, but they always get out, get lost, and die. I know so many mothers who have swept dead little turtles from under a bed or dresser, because the children didn't take care of them properly. The little turtles got hungry because no one fed them, and escaped to look for food, and died. I can't have that."

I swore that I would take the best possible care of a turtle. I swore this so many times that at last Mom agreed to let me have one. But she made a stipulation. I had to promise that I would study the tank of turtles at Woolworth's for a long time (no doubt while she did her Woolworth's shopping in peace), so I could choose the strongest, healthiest turtle in the tank.

One cold spring Saturday we drove to Twin Falls together: Mom, my baby sister Vicki, who was two and a half, and I. We did other shopping, and then, at long last, entered Woolworth's. I raced to the back of the store, headed for the pet shelves near the side door, while Mother and Vicki went off together. I stood at the turtle tank and studied the little fellows swimming so gallantly, each trying to haul out of the water by climbing onto the back of the next one. They were red-eared sliders, I know now, and each silver-dollar-sized turtle was marked with a red stripe on each side of the neck behind the eye. I stared at them with deep satisfaction. One of these baby turtles would soon be mine and I was determined to get a good one, to get the very best baby turtle in the tank.

A few minutes later, this seemed an impossible task. All the baby turtles looked identical, and if I found an especially vigorous one, I soon failed to track him in the swimming mass of his brothers and had to start over. But, suddenly, I realized that one was different.

This fellow was darker, stockier. And—yes, it was true! He had no red stripes on his neck. I studied this one with care as he swam around the tank. He was strong. His shell was smooth and undamaged. Underneath, his shell was bright yellow, patterned with intricate marks of dark green and almost-black, unlike the ventral tracings of the others. He was the one! Trembling with eagerness, I gave the bored young clerk instructions, and after many tries, at last he captured my special turtle. "They are all alike, kid!" the gum-snapping, pimply clerk said during the capture attempts. "They are just the same. Look, I have a nice one in the net right now." But undaunted, I held out for the stocky, dark one that wore no red stripes. At last he swam into the net and was placed in the white cardboard box with the wire handle, as if he were a sort of Chinese take-out delicacy. I chose a habitat bowl and tin of ant eggs and gave the clerk my $2.00. Mother and Vicki returned, and as we drove home in the early twilight, I clutched the cardboard box with clenched hands. *My turtle.*

That night the baby turtle was placed in his habitat on the night stand in the bedroom, between my bed and Vicki's, and I shook in some unappetizing brown flakes from the turtle food can. The turtle looked at the brown specks, made a few nips at them, and spat them out. "He will get the idea," I thought, and turned out the light. I slept well.

The next morning there was no turtle. Frantic, and desperate not to be like the bad children who had let their turtles die, I searched our bedroom and finally found my turtle under the bed, stultified in lint. I rinsed him under the bathroom tap and put him back into the habitat and fed him more dried ant eggs. And he ignored them and escaped. And I put him back in. And he escaped.

This wasn't going to work. I raided the refrigerator for a pinch of hamburger and made it into tiny balls and offered them. He spurned them and escaped once more, bouncing off the dresser, landing bravely on the cotton rug between our beds. I put him back into the habitat yet again. An idea occurred to me. I knew that toads would take only moving food. Was it the same with turtles? I took a short length of thread from Mother's sewing box and pinched a tiny bit of hamburger to one end as I had learned to do for my baby toads of the previous summer. Carefully, I trailed this through the water past the little turtle's nose. He made a grab, bit, and swallowed as I pulled the thread free. This was going to work. A few minutes later, stuffed with raw hamburger, the turtle climbed onto his island, pulled in his legs, and slept under the warmth of the little lamp there.

Mother came into the bedroom to see if we were awake. "I see that your turtle is sleeping," she said. "Has he eaten?"

"Yes, he has," I replied proudly.

"Good," Mom said. "What are you going to name him?" She knew that to me naming was a kind of magic.

I had given it considerable thought, and his behavior on this early Sunday morning had decided me on his true name. "His name is Crusader," I said, and it sounded right.

"Crusader Turtle!" my mother echoed as if taken aback. "That's a big name for such a small animal."

I took him into my hand and held him up to her. "He's brave," I said, "like a knight. He doesn't give up. He has a coat of armor. And," I said, turning him so she could see his underside, "he bears his coat of arms on his shield." For Christmas I had received a book about King Arthur and the knights of the Round Table and had read it over and over.

To my surprise, Mother put a hand to her cheek and left the room. But Crusader Turtle he was and Crusader Turtle he remained.

Crusader ate hamburger, he ate lettuce, he ate worms, he ate baked potato, he ate spinach, and he ate bits of steak. He escaped from his plastic habitat many times, until a friend gave me a cracked five-gallon aquarium for him. But Crusader still spent a good part of his day trying to escape. As spring warmed into summer, school let out, and often I would take Crusader with me on my rambles into the nearby hills and fields. I would put him on the ground and let him feel dirt beneath his feet. Then back he would go into my shirt pocket, home to his tank.

Mother found a little field guide to reptiles and amphibians on another shopping trip to Twin. Just like every field guide I saw in those days, it was written for eastern North America. There was never a field guide to anything available for the West. But Crusader's family was from the East. Mom placed the book in my hands, and I turned to the turtles at once. And there, on page 12, was Crusader. He was a False-Map Turtle! A map turtle. No wonder he felt driven to explore.

Crusader lived in his tank for several years and attained a shell length of three inches. He began to grow long front toenails, proving that he was, indeed, a male. I would swear that he knew me. Crusader's green-and-cream head would slide from his shell at my step into the bedroom, and he would look into my face with his cold yellow eye. "Got any hamburger?" was probably what he was thinking, but I knew there was something else. Crusader wanted adventure. He craved great deeds of daring and he wanted freedom. He was a small knight-errant caged in a tank. He never tired of trying to escape.

There were two vacant lots between my house and my friend Tommy's house. These lots were paradise to the neighborhood children, covered as they were with sagebrush, tall wild rye, and a profusion of wildflowers. Strangely, long, straight ditches ran through these lots in a kind of grid pattern, dry ditches. We loved to play hide and seek, running bent-over and invisible in the ditches, and finding hiding places where the grass hung down thickly over the ditch banks and made little caves. We had to take great care when running that we didn't fall into the ditches, but that was fine. We knew them all by heart. Many years later I came across an old photo of Ketchum, 1890s vintage, and solved the mystery of our childhood ditches. The lots had once been part of a small farm, complete with irrigation ditches. No matter; Ketchum's Community Library stands there now, covering both lots. The ditches are gone.

Behind Tommy's fence line, near where his grandpa parked their pickup, a big pipe came straight up from the ground. The pipe was large, perhaps eight inches in diameter, topped with a black iron cap. It came up about four inches from the level of the ground, and just below the cap was a long, vertical crack.

The pipe leaked. Tommy dug out the dirt all around the pipe, to a depth of about two feet, and soon he had a small pond. The pond, four feet in diameter, was a favorite play spot for us children. Tommy's little pond soon sported muddy child-tracks all around, and a variety of plastic boats and other toys. We would hide them in a big clump of wild rye when we had finished playing there for the day and retrieved them the next time. From the pond, a narrow trail of water followed one of the ditches for almost a hundred feet, where it pooled in a little hollow. This pond was smaller but deeper, overgrown with tall grasses and partly shaded by a bent sagebrush.

I took Crusader to Tommy's pond nearly every day that summer. Crusader did well in the pond. He swam, he dived, he was made to ride on plastic boats, he tried to dig in the mud and hide. At the end of the play time, I would swish him in the water to clean off his shell, and he would go home to his tank. Now when I put my hand down for him in the tank, he would rush eagerly to me. Turtles have some understanding of activity sequencing. I knew he hoped he would go to the pond.

But autumn came, and ice, and cold, and snow. Once more Crusader was confined to his tank in the bedroom. He came to my hand with less and less eagerness as the winter months wore on, but he always came. And he never stopped trying to escape.

I took Crusader to Tommy's pond the first day that the ice

was all gone. He ran to the edge of the water as fast as turtles can run and launched himself over the ten-inch cliff we had made for him. Splash! Though the water was cold, Crusader swam and swam and had to be caught from the water to go home when it began to get dark. We went to the pond often.

One warm summer night I was alone there, lying full-length in the grass, watching Crusader swim in circles as the last light of an orange sunset faded from the sky and from the water. I knew what I should do. I got up, dusted my knees, and left him there.

I was up with the sun and ran to Tommy's pond. There was Crusader, sunning on the bank, just like a real turtle would do at a real pond. I didn't want to leave him there during the day. What if one of the other kids stole him? Or stepped on him? What if Tommy's grandpa ran over him with the pickup when he went to work? So I took Crusader home.

That summer Crusader spent many nights at the pond. I would take care to be the last one there before dark and the first one there in the morning, to keep him safe. He grew stronger and larger, with an unblemished, glossy shell and snapping yellow eyes. And one morning when I came to get him, Crusader was gone.

Heartsick, I searched in widening circles around the pond. I even probed the mud at the bottom with a willow branch and felt all along the banks under water. He was gone. Then I thought of the little trickle in the ditch. After all, he was an explorer, a map turtle far from his own country.

I found him in the little pool where the water ended, the one overgrown with grass and shaded by the bent sagebrush. He came to my outstretched hand, but when I closed my fingers, tried to scurry away. I let him go and thought for some time. I was twelve years old, and for me, too, the world was wider than it had been when I was just eight and he was a silver-dollar baby. This pool was in the south half of the empty lot. I had never seen any of the other children here. Perhaps they didn't know about it. It was far from roads and the place where Tommy's grandfather parked the pickup. Long grasses trailed in the water and made good hiding places for a small creature, just like the overgrown dry ditches made good hiding places for us children. "Well, Crusader," I said to him. "I hope you like your new home."

I went to Crusader's pool almost every day that summer, and usually found him there. Once I found him fifty feet away in the sagebrush, walking rapidly through the grasses, a blue flower caught between one front leg and his shell, like the token of a lady given to her true knight to bring him luck in the jousts. I wanted to take him back to his pool, but he looked so formidable and so knowing, that I stepped to one side and let him continue on his way. The next day he was back at the pool. I hoped he found great deeds to perform, but I thought he must be lonely. Every time we went to Twin, I begged to go to Woolworth's. Once there, I searched the turtle tank for another false map turtle. I searched for years, but never found him a friend or a lady.

School started that September, and one morning there was ice on the grass under the sprinklers on our front lawn. I freshened the tank and went to get Crusader. He was sunning on the bank, and when I came, plopped into the water and disappeared for a long time. Feeling under the water, I found that he had dug a neat turtle-sized hole in the mud of the bank and was hiding there. I came away without him, thoughtful.

A few weeks later Mom said, "It's supposed to snow tonight. Hadn't you better get Crusader in for the winter? His kind are from the south. There aren't any turtles here in Idaho because it's too cold in the winter for them. You had better go right after school."

She was right. A winter at 6,000 feet would kill him. "Yes, Mom," I said.

QUINNEY

After school I walked home through the empty lot and stood for a long time looking down at the dark water of Crusader's pool. He was nowhere to be found. I knew he was in his burrow in the cold mud. I knew just where to put my hand to reach him. And yet . . .

The first snowflakes of the year began to fall. I felt them on my face and hands, and I knew how cold it would be in Ketchum in the winter, and how long the dark would be, and how bitter. But he was *Crusader*. I left him there.

The next morning a foot of snow flattened the tall grasses and covered the bent sage, the small pond, and the ditch. I cleaned Crusader's tank and carried it to the basement. And through the winter I thought about him during the 30-below-zero nights, and the sparkling ice-hard days, and the dim afternoons of wind and drifting snow. And I was sorry.

As soon as the snow melted in the spring, I went to Crusader's pool, but Crusader was not there. I went every day after school for weeks, but didn't find him, and more than once I cried hot tears. It had been a mistake to leave him for the winter, but now it was too late for regret. Mother offered to buy me another turtle. But, no. There would never be another Crusader. I was just like the bad children who let their turtles die under the bed in balls of lint. I had failed him.

Summer grew hot, the mosquitoes came in waves, we went on picnics, we children played hide and seek in the empty lot, and we went for long walks beyond the Fourhills, all the way to Lake Creek. I checked Crusader's pool now and then, but he was gone.

It was the Fourth of July, and I had a quarter in my pocket, on my way to the drug store for an ice-cream cone. Just to save time, I cut through the empty lot and ran through the tall grasses near Crusader's pool. Suddenly I heard a *splash*! It stopped me dead in my tracks. Cautiously I approached the pool. There in the water was Crusader!

I lifted him and looked into his bright little eye. His shell was scratched across. Perhaps a dog had tried to take him, who could tell? But he was alive and healthy. I brought Mom to see him, and we stood watching him make lunch out of mosquito larvae when they came to the surface of the pool to breathe. "Well, he's in his element, isn't he?" she said.

I came to see him often, and brought my books to read there at times, fitting my head and shoulders into the low shade of the bent sagebrush. Once in a great while Crusader would haul out of the pond and come to bask next to me. Sometimes I brought him little bits of hamburger pinched to the end of a thread. These were good times. I never told the other children that Crusader was living free. Crusader and me; that's the way it was.

When winter came again, he disappeared into the mud once more. And in the summer, I would sometimes see him at the pool, sometimes not, and thought of him as a lone knight-errant gone on a quest, but always returning at length to his castle keep.

I went through high school, and Crusader remained at his pool. I went away to college, but when I came home for the summer each year, I would often see Crusader, now grown to four inches across the shell, sunning at his pond. The summer I graduated from college, I saw him a few times and shared a hot-dog sandwich with him one afternoon. But then, married, I moved away.

Sometime during the years when I was away, the city bought the two empty lots, cleared them of sage, wild rye, and wildflowers, and built the library there. When I came home after that, I saw Crusader no more. I learned more about turtles, and found that false-map turtles range as far north as Wisconsin, where winters can be quite terrible. So perhaps it was no wonder that Crusader survived. But I'm sure his strong spirit had something to do with it. I wish I knew what happened to him when they built the library, but I think I know.

Did the bulldozers crush him? I will never know for certain. I like to think that when the nearby soil was disturbed by the great, vibrating monsters, Crusader set out to find a new kingdom. Though it has been more than fifty years since I last saw Crusader, I know that turtles live long. It's possible that to this day he lives somewhere in that high, cold valley. After all, it was less than two hundred yards from his pool to Trail Creek, a very good place for a turtle.

When I think of him, I see Crusader striding bravely through the wild grasses with a larkspur flower caught between one front leg and his shell, like the token of a lady. On his shield he bears a strange and mysterious device, the coat of arms of his kind, bound for the quest, knight-errant, clad in armor.

Sonata

We were buying a piano! The piano was a used upright, painted black. It had three pedals, a bench with a maroon cushion that actually lifted up to reveal a storage area for sheet music, and it cost a hundred and twenty-five dollars.

I was nine years old, and Mom thought it high time for me to learn an instrument. "The piano is the thing to learn, Danny," she would say, very serious over cookies and milk when I came home from school. "When you are older and know the piano well, you can play for sing-along parties and invite all your friends. It will be wonderful."

Doubtful, I would look at her across the table without saying much. I had few friends, and I could not imagine being the center of fun at the sort of parties she was describing. They sounded alien to me. It took me a long time to think about these parties as something desirable. After some time, however, I got into the proper spirit. Maybe the piano would be my key to popularity. I loved to sing, and very much liked to sing to the piano at school when Mrs. McMonigal played it during music time. Gradually I began to warm to the idea, but I had reservations.

"What I would really like is something like a guitar, that I could carry with me and sing to in the hills when I am by myself writing songs," I would say. "Or how about voice lessons?" But Mother would invariably come back to the piano as the only possible instrument for a little girl like me. I began to believe her.

"Now, we won't spend all this money on the piano unless you promise to practice every day," Mom would say. "You must be serious about this, because we will have to pay for lessons." And so, eventually, I promised. And I thought I was serious about the piano.

I was even a little excited when the big, blocky piano was delivered to our door and Daddy and Gramps wrestled it into Mom and Dad's bedroom, the only place where there was room for it. I sat on the bench and plonked a few keys with my hand. Could I do this? Would it turn out to be fun? Maybe I could. Maybe it would.

Very soon I was enrolled as one of Mrs. McBride's after-school piano pupils. Mrs. McBride lived several miles south of town, so each Wednesday after school, instead of walking the three blocks home, I would board the school bus and get off with Mrs. McBride's son at the square log cabin near the shale mountain and would take my lesson. Afterward, Mom would drive south to pick me up, eagerly asking questions, wanting to know everything about what I had learned.

I was abysmal at piano. I am sure, even after this long space of years, that Mrs. McBride would remember me as one of her worst. Oh, dear! I learned the notes and the fingering for my level, but I unfortunately had two handicaps. One was a very poor sense of timing. I came to hate the sharp little metronome Mrs. McBride invariably placed on the piano when I sat down for my lesson. It fought me and I fought it, except on those frequent occasions when I forgot about the metronome entirely.

And even worse were my hands themselves–small, star-shaped, and short-fingered. My fingers would almost reach an octave, almost, if I spread them so wide that it hurt. But not quite. My fingers remained stubby and chubby through two years of weekly piano lessons. My mundane little fingers would not arch gracefully. They would not point the keys with delicacy, and they just would not reach the spans they needed to reach.

I told myself that I was giving piano a very good try, but that became less and less true as the second year of my lessons dragged on. I cut my daily practices at home as short as I could. During lessons, I would often stare out Mrs. McBride's window beyond the black and white keys. I would look away across the road to the steep shale hill and its rock outcrops and dark fir trees. Maybe foxes lived there. Perhaps today I would see some deer crossing the slope. Maybe anything would happen if I pretended that I was not having my piano lesson. I suppose it is something of a miracle that Mrs. McBride didn't find a way to murder me.

I began to hate the piano, at first secretly, and finally with an open, sullen hatred. Mom was hopelessly outdated. Pianos as party tools were out and hi-fis were in. Young people didn't sing along to the piano anymore; they gathered to play records or listen to top forty hits on the radio. And even if the piano had been the hottest fun-generator since the swimming pool, I could not imagine inviting classmates home to hear me stumble through the idiotic little pieces assigned to me.

At the end of that year of lessons, sometime during the Christmas holidays, Mrs. McBride held an evening recital of her pupils, me included. I played an unchallenging piece that had a little word song with it, that went, "Stately as princes the swans part the lilies and glide under the willows," which for some reason seared itself into my brain so well that I remember it after many decades. The piece had two-handed fingering, and I could actually play it. But not with heart and not with grace. I made my way through the recital like a sleepwalker. Mother knew that I really wasn't there at all.

Still, she tried. She tried shame, she tried rewards, she tried punishments, she tried freedom from chores, all to get me to put in my practice. But I was eleven now, and as stubborn as her own father, my Gramps. I was shutting down and backing out. Sometimes at night when sleep was close, I would see in the blackness a ghost image—the dark cliff of the piano looming over my bed like a squared-off troll with many teeth. If I had known magic, I would have vanished it, regardless of the hundred and twenty-five dollars. I had thoughts about hatchets and kindling, and especially about matches.

Then came the day that I did not get on the school bus on Wednesday night, but walked deliberately, warily home, knowing that I was a very bad girl. With tears already running down my cheeks, I opened the door to our house and took myself into the bright kitchen. When Mom saw me, I could tell she was very, very angry, but all she said was, "Go to your room." I felt terrible, and the piano saw me as I passed through the short hall to my bedroom, black as an unscalable mountain, a silent monster condemning me.

After a dinner which I did not get to eat, Mom came in and sat down on the bed beside me. "We did this for you, Danny," she said. "You promised. And now you seem to hate it. But the piano is wonderful. It's a doorway to many beautiful things."

"I do hate it," I said with the frank cruelty of children, at last able to say the words to her. "If you think the piano is so wonderful, why don't you learn to play it yourself?"

"Go to bed," Mom replied, and left me.

I cried myself to sleep that night. But the next afternoon when I came home after school, my music workbook had been put away and the piano key-cover was closed. We did not speak of the piano for weeks after that, and I cut it dead, pretending it had ceased to exist. After a month or two, I forgot to be oppressed by its presence.

Winter passed. The new grass came up green on the Fourhills behind our house, and I spent hours there searching for flowers. Also, I was playing softball after school, and doing well. I was the catcher on our impromptu neighborhood team. Life was just fine.

One afternoon I had just come into the house through the side porch, tossing my softball glove onto a chair, when I heard something familiar. I held so still that I almost lost my balance. There it came, a soft, tinkling tune, and I knew the words. "Stately as princes the swans part the lilies and glide under the willows. Are they enchanted men soon to be free again here, under the willows? Oh, I would like to be here when a fairy wand touches the leader and changes his looks. Would he be handsome and brave as the heroes that live hidden in my fairy books?" Haltingly, but with a light touch I had never possessed, Mother was playing the piano.

Mom kept at it. She used my lesson books, and practiced every spare moment. By midsummer she had stopped hiding her practices and began buying sheet music for popular tunes, and we sang together around the piano many nights—Mom, little Vicki, and I—a very small but very merry party. That summer seemed to pass quickly, and when school rolled around again in September, I remember thinking that now Mom would have more time to practice, since Vicki and I wouldn't be around the house as much.

One Saturday in December I had been out with camera and snowshoes during a feathery, snowy day walking over the snow-buried sagebrush near Penny Mountain. By late afternoon I was cold and wet and very tired and looked forward to the warm house and perhaps a cup of hot cocoa before dinner. By the time I reached our door it was dark. The snow had stopped, and the stars were coming out between wisps of disappearing cloud. Over Dollar Mountain, a lopsided moon sailed through the torn clouds, and the sky was indigo ink.

I stopped still in the doorway. The house was filled with music, piano notes rippling exquisitely through the air. Mother

My mother, Bernice, was an expert fly fisherwoman,
but didn't fish as often as Dad.

was playing a piece I had never heard before. I stepped through the door and was engulfed in the sound, sweet beyond imagining. I forgot I was cold and stood dripping until the last note died away.

Mom came from the bedroom and saw me.

"What was that?" I asked.

"It's called the *Moonlight Sonata*," she said. "Beethoven."

I sat right down on the floor in my snow clothes. "That's your piano now," I said.

Mom sat on the floor beside me and began to help me pull off my boots. "I guess it has been my piano all along, Danny," she said. "You know, when I was your age I dearly wanted a piano and lessons. My brother got a saxophone and saxophone lessons. But I was only a girl. Things were different for girls in those days."

I shed my wet coat and mittens, and we went into the kitchen for hot cocoa.

As the months and years rolled by, Mother found Chopin, Bartok, Liszt, and many others. Mom often played the pieces by heart with her eyes closed, with no sheet music on the stand, her long, tapering fingers arched delicately over the keys, sitting enchanted at her piano.

The Anthology

In 1953, I was nine years old, and I was a reader. It wasn't easy to be a voracious reader in Ketchum, Idaho, in the 1950s. Our small town had no library and no bookstore. As could be said of almost every commodity, books could be bought in Twin Falls, a city 85 miles to the south. But in our family, money had to go for food and clothing, doctor bills, gasoline, electricity, and the like. There was little money for books.

The only place in town that was a library was a room in the Ketchum Grade School, the only school, where children went from first through eighth grade. Most of the books were, to my mind, very old, and there were few books, perhaps 5,000 in all. I read them, nevertheless. "Went through them like a buzz saw" was what my mother said. I would get a book or two for my birthday or for Christmas, and I would read them into tatters. Dad brought home all the unclaimed paperbacks that tourists would leave behind on Sun Valley resort's ski buses. But they weren't enough.

One hot July day Mom was running errands and I went down to the grade school with my bag of marbles. Soon I was playing marbles by myself on the school sidewalk, the only sidewalk in our half of town. I smelled smoke and trotted around the side of the school building to find the source. In the inside corner made from the two wings of the building, the school janitor was burning books.

A rusty fifty-gallon drum shot flames four feet into the air, and gouts of cauliflower smoke puffed out every time he dropped in a book. I was outraged. He was burning books, when I wanted them so much, so much.

"Stop, mister!" I shouted, heading for the barrel at a dead run. "You can't burn those books!"

With a tight smile, the janitor dusted his gloved hands together and leaned on a rake with a broken handle. Smiling, he told me that yes, he very well could burn the books. In fact, he had been ordered by the departing principal to burn all the textbooks more than ten years old. With this, he dropped in a few more books and stirred them around with the blackened end of his rake handle. I stood near stacks of books on the ground and looked at him, for once speechless. Smoke stung my eyes.

Averting his own eyes, the janitor said, "Well, some of these books could disappear. I am going to keep on burning them, but if some git gone, well they would be gone no matter where they went, wouldn't they? It would save me hauling some ashes, little girl."

I saw his face as he dropped in another book. No amount of pleading would move him simply to stop burning the books, so I decided that action was the thing. Pawing madly through the stacks of books on the ground, I saw that most of them were in sets of 20 or more identical textbooks, mostly reading texts. I grabbed one each of these until I could hold no more, and ran toward home, a very hard uphill two blocks with such a heavy load.

Dumping the books onto the grass beside our front steps, I reached for the long black handle of my red Radio Flyer wagon and flew down the hill to the school, wagon wheels bouncing and shimmying behind me on the dirt road, a cloud of dust billowing in our wake like a long, fluffy tail.

Breathless, I arrived just in time to see the janitor drop

another book into the burn barrel; he smiled again. I knew my time was limited. At any moment it might amuse him to stop me and send me on my way. I scrabbled among the books and loaded them into the wagon, trying hard to get at least one of each kind.

At last I had jammed and piled and fitted as many books as I could get into and onto my Radio Flyer. Moving very slowly, with one hand on the towering wagonload of books, I pulled the Flyer home.

When Mom got home from her errands, she was astonished to find me enthroned in books on the shady side of the house, reading and sipping grape Kool-Aid. My back against the siding, I sat on the grass with legs extended, and the wide "arms" of my "chair" were made of books, dozens of them.

"Danny!" she exclaimed. "Where did you get these?"

"At the school," I told her. "The janitor is burning books today, and he said I could take as many as I could carry."

"Burning books," she said. Mom lifted a small, shabby book with a tan cloth cover from the arm of my throne. "Oh!" she said when she turned the book over, so startled she almost dropped it. She sat down on the grass and held it out to me. On the cover was a rabbit dressed in clothes, and the title, stamped in black, was *The Field First Reader*.

"Danny," Mother said. "This was my very first reader when I was in the first grade in Gooding Grade School. I loved this book."

"You keep that one," I said. "I'm glad it didn't get burned."

Mother held *The Field First Reader* to her cheek. "I'm glad, too," she said. "It has been a long time since I've seen one of these fellows." Something in her face changed and she left me, marching up the concrete steps into the house and banging the screen door. I had been told many times never to bang the screen door.

After a few moments, I heard Mother's voice on the phone.

The only word that came to me through the open window was, "Never." I heard her say, "Never, never," the way she said things when she meant them. The next day, the stack of books near the burn barrel was gone, and the janitor was nowhere to be seen. I never saw anyone burn books at the school again.

For days, for weeks and months, I was lost in stories, myths, and poems from the old textbooks. I learned what happened in "The Wreck of the Hesperus," and "For Want of a Nail," and all about "The Death of Baldur." I discovered how Perseus rescued Andromeda, and why Demeter went weeping for her child and made the winters bleak, and how fine it is "When the Frost is on the Punkin'." All these were things not found in my own schoolbooks. I was astonished to find that *The Field First Reader* would have been suitable for me and my classmates in the fourth grade, much too difficult for first graders at our school.

I still have several of those rescued books. Some were damaged twenty years ago in a flooded basement. Some were given to friends. But still on my shelf in the kitchen are *The Field First Reader* and the book about Baldur and Loki, Perseus and Andromeda, Demeter and Proserpina, and Pluto.

Not long after the incident with the burn barrel, a number of ladies met over coffee, ladies intent upon a certain project. These "library ladies," as they came to be called, invented a second-hand store called "The Gold Mine." This was the plan: everyone would go door to door asking for donated items of any description, and the sale of these things would eventually result in a real library for our town.

Someone found a very old two-room log cabin with a small wood stove, and rented it for $25 a month. Someone else knocked together some rough tables from used lumber. And on a weathered board, our friend Annette Castle painted a miner panning gold, with the words, "The Gold Mine" lettered over his head. This sign was nailed above the door of the cabin.

The library ladies took turns collecting items, washing them, tagging them with prices, laying them out on the rough tables, and clerking the store. At first the things that came in were worn-out pots and pans, shirts with frayed cuffs, curling leather boots, and costume jewelry with missing rhinestones. But the library ladies did not give up. Then actress Ann Southern donated a box. From her box came a beautiful white full skirt hand-painted with holly leaves and spangled with clusters of red sequins. Mom bought that skirt for a dollar, and I twirled in Saks Fifth Avenue on Christmas Eve. Then Norma Shearer biked to the Gold Mine with a basket of exquisitely tailored slacks and blouses to donate. Business at the Gold Mine became brisk.

Not long after that, the Gold Mine became "the thing." No longer were most of the donations faded and worn. Wealthy part-time residents gave boxes overflowing with stunningly beautiful, nearly new items like my white Saks Fifth Avenue skirt. Us Campfire Girls went door to door once a month collecting. People liked our fresh faces and gave good things. Suddenly everyone was shopping the Gold Mine. The library ladies moved the Gold Mine to a larger cabin, and marked up the prices on the tags. Money came in. Plans for a building were drawn. Truckloads of bricks and lumber arrived at the site. Foundations were poured. Ketchum really was going to have a library!

Walls went up, doors and windows went in, floors went down, and shelf upon shelf upon shelf went up. Someone donated a new encyclopedia. Someone else donated tables and chairs. Boxes and boxes of donated books, yet to be unpacked, waited in the back room. A big desk was manhandled sideways through the door and was placed at one end of the room. "Ketchum Public Library," said a new sign above the door, and the library was only three blocks from our house!

School was let out early on the afternoon that the library

opened, and many of the children raced to the library to claim library cards, the first library cards we had ever owned. Mine was number 12.

Mrs. Lucille Conley was hired as Ketchum's first librarian. Everyone liked Mrs. Conley. I remember her pencil-slim straight skirts and crisp white blouses with short sleeves and Peter Pan collars, but mostly I remember her shining dark hair, arched brows, and beautiful, heavily lashed eyes. Mrs. Conley was serious about books, and I liked that, too. I was twelve years old, and I volunteered to help her unpack and catalogue the books. She agreed that I could come in and work with her for an hour after school several times a week.

The first time I worked at the library is lost to me now; I simply do not remember. But not long after the books were on the shelves and the doors open to the public, came a day I will never forget.

Book donations were still coming in, boxes and boxes of them. Some boxes were stuffed full of dull volumes of ancient sermons. Some donations were small boxes of paperbacks with bright covers so lurid that Mrs. Conley whisked them away from me the moment the boxes were opened. Other boxes contained old school texts like the ones I had rescued from the burn barrel.

One evening after school I joined Mrs. Conley in the back room, where she was opening still more cardboard boxes of books. She had taken off her high heels, and her feet were neat in nylon stockings as she kneeled over the latest donations. "Lyle Jolley" had been scrawled across the tops of several boxes.

"Look, Danny," Mrs. Conley said, holding up a book. "Here are the very first poetry books for our library. Robert Louis Stevenson, Henry Wadsworth Longfellow!" She piled them carefully to one side on the floor. "And here are some ancient writings: Aristotle, Thucydides. This is good stuff. Here, you finish this box and I'll open the next one."

As my fingers closed around a slim volume titled *The Odyssey*, Mrs. Conley said, "A young couple brought these boxes in this afternoon. These were found in her uncle's house in Jerome after he died, and no one in the family wanted them. They said he died without children, all alone, and left a little house and very little else except these books. And they are good ones!" She opened the flyleaf of one book. "Lyle Jolley," it read. "I'll bet Mr. Jolley would like to know that his books ended up in the library here where we so desperately need good books," she said. I put *The Odyssey* on Mrs. Conley's pile.

I lifted out the next book, a weighty volume bound in red cloth. It fell open at a poem by Lord Byron. I didn't know who Byron was, but I remember the line: "The Assyrian came down like the wolf on the fold . . ." I went away into the verse, as I did then, as I do to this day.

"Danny," Mrs. Conley was saying. "Danny? Danny, what is it that you have?" Carefully, she lifted the book from my hands and read the title aloud:

"*Anthology of Romanticism*," she read. "Oh, look! It's all the romantic poets—Byron, Keats, Shelley, Wordsworth—nearly all their works! What a wonderful book to have in our library." Then her face fell as she turned it over. "Oh, dear," she went on. "What a shame. The back's broken and there's a big three-cornered tear in the fabric of the back cover. What a shame," she repeated. "This book is too damaged to go into the library. It would just fall apart."

Briskly, Mrs. Conley got to her feet and slipped into her high heels. She looked down at me. "You know," she said, "I hate to throw this book away. Might you want it, Danny? If you do, it's yours."

I hope I thanked her, but I don't remember. Clutching the heavy book in both hands, I stumbled out the door and ran all the way home. I didn't sleep much that night, nor the next. The

Romantic poets were mine!

The Anthology went to school in my bag. It came out at lunchtime and had tuna salad and potato chips dropped into its pages. *The Anthology* was shoved into saddlebags and was read in every gulch and canyon within a dozen miles of Ketchum. Mud and dust stained it, grass and leaves and rain. Each year the pages got a little looser, but the stitching held; *The Anthology* never fell apart. Sometimes I would trace the signature on the flyleaf, *Lyle Jolley*, and think of Mr. Jolley alone in his house in Jerome, reading this book, looking at the sun setting far across the fields and gazing toward the dim outlines of mountains to the north and to the southeast—and I would wonder what he had thought, what he had looked like, and above all, why his family had not wanted his books.

The Anthology went camping; it went on vacation to California, it sat beside the stove while I cooked, it lay open on the ironing board, it went to college, it went to work, it was packed into another cardboard box and moved thousands of miles, and moved again, and again. Its torn red cover faded even more. The tape I had used to mend the tear on the back cover turned brittle and fell away. And the tape that I used on the next repair cracked with age and came off, and the next, and the next.

I must move again, to a new house some distance away, and now must begin to pack my books for the first time in years. For fifteen years *The Anthology* has stood in the middle of the bookcase in the kitchen corner. A few puppy teeth have worried the edges, but not a single page has fallen. "Lyle Jolley" can still be read on the flyleaf.

I will pack *The Anthology* soon, but for the most part, I no longer need to read it. I can see the words; I can hear them and I can say them: "The Assyrian came down like the wolf on the fold; His cohorts were gleaming in purple and gold . . ."

I will unpack *The Anthology* in the new house and it will

stand in the middle of a bookcase in the kitchen, as it does here now, unlikely treasure. Lyle Jolley's legacy has been with me most of my life and has colored the way I have seen the world. Thank you, Mrs. Conley. Thank you, Mr. Jolley, whoever you were.

There are children of the body, and there are children of the mind. Lyle Jolley had no children, but though I never met him, I am his child. I have no children, and I wonder, when the shadow falls upon me, if there will be someone to take this collection of dreams and carry it into the future. It's just an old book, hard-used, shabby, stained, dog-eared, and patched with tape, too damaged to be accepted by a library. I very much hope that someone will treasure *The Anthology* as I have. Perhaps I should add "D. Stewart Quinney" to the flyleaf before I go.

The Assyrian came down like the wolf on the fold,
And his cohorts were gleaming in purple and gold,
And the sheen of their spears was like stars on the sea,
Where the blue wave rolls nightly o'er brave Galilee.
—Byron

The Fairy

The three of us snuggled into our sleeping bags and looked up into the deep black of a late-August sky. We had drunk our fill of cherry Kool-Aid, and it was time to giggle, watch for falling stars, and talk about all manner of girl things.

The upcanyon wind that blew all day had turned over, and the downcanyon wind brought cool air from the Boulder Mountains and from the Summit Creek country, ruffling the aspen and cottonwood leaves two blocks away along Trail Creek. Summer was old and was passing. School loomed, a cloud barely visible on the distant horizon, a thought to be banished from consciousness every time it surfaced.

We three were the only grade-school girls in our part of town, and that had made us friends: Sally, twelve; Emily, eight; and me, ten going on eleven. This summer we had inner-tubed the river, made picnics for our dolls, caught innumerable tadpoles and frogs, constructed little ranches for our plastic cowboys and horses, swum in the downtown pool at Bald Mountain Hot Springs, collected pockets full of jasper and agate, played softball and hide-and-go-seek, sat in the shade reading piles of comic books, sewed doll clothes, tried on makeup when our mothers were gone, pretended we were pirates (and Lewis and Clark and Sacajawea, and knights with swords, and Robin Hood, and pioneer women, and cowboys and Indians, and the Three Musketeers, and the Lone Ranger, and movie stars).

We had gone camping with our families, worked at keeping our homes neat, watered lawns, weeded gardens, lugged home heavy bags of groceries, washed family cars, and given our dogs their baths. We had done all the summer things that not-so-very-little girls do when they are in their independent, largely pre-boy, top of childhood competence.

On this warm night, we lay in our sleeping bags on the back lawn at my house. It was dark as dark. Mom had left the light on over the front porch for us just in case we needed to come in during the night, but our sleeping bags lay around two corners of the house from the porch light, and we couldn't see even the faintest glow from any light but the stars as we lay in the dark grass.

Our street was a dirt road without sidewalks and streetlamps. Few cars passed by and almost none after ten at night. The night was quiet and tranquil, and at 6,000 feet in the 1950s, as clear as a summer night could be. We felt very close to the stars.

My mother had provided a frosty pitcher of red Kool-Aid, chiming with ice, and we had drunk it all, snacking on M&Ms and bananas at the same time. Feeling comfortably full, we watched the occasional meteors fall, streaking across our window of black sky. My brown-and-white-spotted rat terrier, Puppy, had curled up next to me. His soft muzzle rested on my arm, and his warm little body pressed close against my side.

Another meteor arced across the sky and fell behind the Fourhills.

"This is just the kind of night when fairies would be out," I said to Sally and Emily.

"Fairies," Sally snorted with a kind of grown-up scorn. "Do you believe in fairies?"

"Well," I replied slowly, "there could be fairies. I don't see why not."

"There's no such thing as a fairy," Sally said with maddening complacency. She liked reminding us that she was the oldest.

94

"My dad said so."

"Yes, that's right." Sally's little sister Emily put in her two cents' worth, siding with Sally. "No such thing as fairies."

"There's lots written about them. Lots of countries have fairy stories. I did a book report on a book called *Fairy Tales from Around the World*. Why would people in different countries have the same kinds of stories if fairies weren't real?" I said.

"Lots of countries have Santa Claus," said Sally with a laugh, "but we know Santa isn't real. Or do you still believe in Santa Claus, too?"

"I know about Santa," Emily put in. "I found out about Santa a long time ago."

"No, I don't believe in Santa anymore," I said quickly. "But I don't know that anybody has proved that there aren't any fairies. There could be fairies. They don't come out during the daytime. They are supposed to be very shy and hide in little secret places and only come out to dance at night. So, fairies could be living right in this yard, but we would never see them."

"That's because there aren't any fairies," said Sally.

I was irritated but not about to give up. "Well, still, there might be. All the stories that tell about them describe them nearly the same. Their bodies are no bigger than a thumb." I warmed to the subject, talking to myself now. "Fairies have a pair of antennas like butterflies. They have beautifully colored wings. They drink nectar and dew from the flowers. They show themselves to one person at a time. They love the moonlight—"

Here Sally interrupted me: "Fairies don't exist, and you can't prove they do. That fairy stuff is all dumb stuff from books. It isn't real, any of it. What you need to do, Danny, is grow up."

"Yes, that's right," little Emily said for the second time. "Grown-ups don't believe in fairies."

I could see that this conversation had gone quite far down the road to "Naa,naa, na naaa, naa, so there," so I said nothing in reply. Truly, I didn't know if fairies were real, but I loved fairy stories and liked to think they might be.

I stared deep into the starry sky. What about growing up? I asked myself. Was this what being grown up was all about—that nothing existed except what you could see and touch every day? Did everyone have to grow up? Would growing up turn me into another kind of being? I thought about it very solemnly and with a shiver.

Being grown up was coming. It was coming like a long freight train with a bright light and a great noise, and after, things would never be the same. I didn't know how not to grow up. Nobody had ever not grown up, not unless they died first.

Beside me I could hear soft, regular breathing. Sally and Emily had fallen asleep. Puppy got up, turned around to make his fur lie the right way, and lay down again on my sleeping bag. I pulled the top layer up to my chin.

What was life if you were a grown-up? Boys and dates, I thought. That comes first. Football games, dances. Putting makeup on and curling your hair. A wedding, children. Shopping. Keeping house. Cooking. Mowing the lawn. Driving. Working. I guessed you could still go camping, have birthday parties, and go to the movies, but that wasn't enough for me. I had never talked to anyone who thought there might be mysteries, or great adventures, or brilliant discoveries out there in grown-up land, even if you were just an ordinary person and not a big hero or anything special. Everything would have to be real, no more pretend. There would be only what you saw and what you did, every single day, no time for dreams and no place for them. I knew I wouldn't like it, but I could see no escape.

On the other hand, I thought, beginning to drift a little on the edge of sleep, what would fairies be like, really? Well, I thought, their clothing would match the colors in their wings. They would make their little shirts and skirts and slippers and leggings and vests and trousers from the finest possible stuff, cobwebs and hummingbird feathers, softer than soft. They would move their wings so silently that no one could hear them flying by. They would have little bright eyes and tiny hands and feet. They would be almost weightless, so they wouldn't leave any tracks at all. They would be very gentle and would not hurt any other creature. At night, light would call to them. They would come out to play in the moonlight or to dance around a fire.

Even so, fairies would be very watchful. They would show themselves only to one person at a time. Before the sun came over the mountain, they would fly away. And no one would be able to follow them home.

I was gone into the night, one of four sleepers, three little girls and a small spotted dog, saved by flannel sleeping bags from cold grass going dewy with the deepening night. It was a long time before I woke up. If I dreamed, I don't remember.

I was awake. To the east over the north shoulder of Dollar Mountain, I saw a grayness that spoke of dawn to come, but the sky overhead was still inky black and full of stars. The Kool-Aid had caught up with me; I had to go into the house to use the bathroom. Gingerly wriggling out of my sleeping bag and hugging myself against goosebumps, I stepped barefoot into the cold, dew-wet grass. Puppy, seizing his opportunity, bolted inside my sleeping bag and disappeared.

Around two corners of the house I trotted, climbed the four chill concrete steps of the porch, and reached for the metal handle of the wood-framed screen door below the porch light.

Twenty inches above my hand, the creature grasped the mesh of the screen with tiny hands and feet. A small body no larger than my thumb clung there under the porch light. His six-inch wings were fantastically colored in rust-red, frosted brown, maroon, and cream, and his body wore a suit of matching colors, made from stuff as delicate as hummingbird feathers. The wings bore downy fringes so soft that no one would ever hear them fluttering as he used them to fly. Two antennae waved gently, questing toward me.

I looked into the small bright eyes and knew his name. "You are a Cecropia moth," I whispered. I had never seen one, only read about them in books. He had come dancing toward the light and had shown himself only to me.

With great care, I opened the screen door and went into the dark house. When I came out minutes later, the fairy had gone. "Still, growing up may have a few surprises," I thought.

The Star of Knob Hill

When I was a girl, early June was a time of morning sunshine, afternoon rain. Each morning, it seemed, began fresh and bright with the previous day's raindrops still gleaming on the wildflowers, grasses, and sagebrush of the Fourhills above our house.

The children who lived in my part of town, right under the hills, had names for each hill. First and lowest was Bluebird Hill, crowned with tilted slabs of pink andesite, where migrating flocks of mountain bluebirds often used as a rest stop in spring and fall. Next was Hungry Plant Hill, whose chief feature was a large split-rock formation that, according to my friend Tommy, looked just like the huge alien plant that almost ate Buck Rogers in the science fiction comic strip in the *Salt Lake Tribune*. Tallest and with the fewest rocks on top (but the best view), was narrow Skyhigh Hill. Finally, there was Jagged Hill, whose entire top was a mass of dark andesite, and whose backside sloped down to the sage-overgrown Ketchum cemetery, where, in the 1950s, no one of world renown yet rested.

I was a flower girl when I was small, and still am to this day. On days when I wasn't in school, each spring morning I went into the Fourhills to look for wildflowers. Our town had few facilities then, and of course there was no internet. Dad told me the names of some of the wildflowers. I had two small pocket guides to flowers, both written for the eastern United States.

Armed with these, I tried to put names to the flowers I found. For many, I had to invent my own names. By the time I was ten, I knew when and where to find each flower of the Fourhills and sought them just to be in their company.

School was now out for the summer, and each morning I would go flower-hunting for a few hours before working at my summer job, watering and weeding lawns and flower beds for part-time residents of my section of town. On this sunny morning, I was searching the lower slopes of Jagged Hill.

Meadowlarks sang from the tops of bitterbrush, the shrubs so laden with yellow blossoms that the world smelled like warm honey. Clutched tightly in one hand I carried a few flowers of what I called Mother's Day violet, along with several of its leaves. I had been given a set of watercolors for my birthday and planned to paint this little yellow violet with the whiskery face and delicate petals. Its leaves, dark green above, were bright maroon on the underside, and as I worked my way southeast across the slope, I wondered how I could paint a view of the plant that would show the underside of a leaf without distorting the rest of the plant.

Walking up the tiny moss-lined runoff draw near the base of Jagged, I turned southwest and worked across the toe of the slope. I crossed the dirt road leading over the small saddle from Mrs. Spiegel's house to the cemetery, eyes on the ground as I searched for flowers. Were the lupine blooming yet? What about the larkspur—were they finished for the year?

In the empty lots behind Mrs. Spiegel's house, the balsamroot was in bloom, as well as the yellow lupine, and the lower hillside blew in alternate waves of silver and green as the undersides of the leaves lifted and fell in the cool wind.

The next hill down was a strange, smooth little hill topped with a fat pillar of dark rock. Everyone in town called it Knob Hill.

Tucked into one flank of Knob Hill were two very small

Arrowleaf balsamroot on the Fourhills.

log cabins, as old and as much alike as brothers, each with a cobblerock chimney. I had never seen anyone go in or out of the lower cabin, and during my night wanderings, had never seen a light coming from its windows. But I knew who lived in the other one. Paulita de Sutter lived there.

Everyone in town knew Paulita, and she knew everyone in town. I was just a little grade-school girl, and one who preferred the company of plants to the company of people, but she knew me; and even I knew who Paulita was.

She was the Paulita de Sutter, and for our town, Paulita provided the drama. With false eyelashes, daringly outrageous dresses, and long stark-white hair, Paulita inserted herself into every event Ketchum and Sun Valley had to offer. No one ever called her "Miss de Sutter." She was always "Paulita." Paulita was old, with wrinkles and clawlike hands, but that didn't stop her from plastering on monumental amounts of makeup or prevent her from wearing a swimsuit in a parade or a gown with breathtaking décolletage to a town meeting. Rumor was that she had been in the movies, way back, before the talkies, even.

Paulita made herself part of every parade, every ceremony, every performance, every meeting. Did she have a job? As a young girl, I didn't know. To me she was simply Paulita.

I had seen her, in high-crowned fur hat and black Astrakhan coat, striding into the post office for her mail, thrusting the door open to let the snowflakes swirl in with her, making an entrance. I had seen her riding in a painted coach in the rodeo parade, looking very non-Western in a white fringed gown and white chiffon scarf, scarlet-tipped fingers toying with a long cigarette holder, silver hair blowing back from her face. I had seen her emerging from Hegstrom's Drugstore with a copy of *Silver Screen Magazine* in one hand and her black cigarette holder in the other, complete with lit cigarette. And just the other day I had seen Paulita, in high heels and a purple chiffon dress, walking downhill on the dirt road to the grocery store, platinum hair streaming down her back. Paulita was an exotic in our small western town, unexpected as an orchid in a garden of pansies. I didn't know what to think of her.

I was looking for a leaf and flower head of waterleaf to take home to paint with my violets, and walked along for some distance, eyes on the ground. Suddenly I smelled smoke and realized with a start that I was very close to Paulita's cabin, close enough to smell the wood smoke drifting up from her chimney. I had come too close and began to move away.

It was too late. A screen door banged open, and oddly, there in the doorway stood my friend Molly, who was one year behind my grade at school. Beside her stood Paulita. "Come on, Danny," Molly said, "Paulita is showing me some stuff."

"Yes, dear, come on in," echoed Paulita. "You're the oldest Stewart girl, aren't you?"

I found my upper arm clutched hard by Paulita's wiry fingers. She dragged at me, and she was strong.

"Come on, Danny," Molly urged me again.

I walked forward and the screen door, followed by a thick wooden door, slammed shut behind us. Inside the cabin it was very warm and smelled of wood smoke and stale perfume. Eventually my eyes adjusted to the dimness.

The place was about the same size as my bedroom. There must have been a bathroom, or even an outhouse, but I don't remember that. I remember coming in from the chill, patchy sunshine into a small room dominated by a bed and a mirror. The bed was covered in an oversized cream satin spread, smoothly puddling on the floor.

At the other end of the room squatted the kind of potbellied stove that has a flat top and two round lids, and beside it crouched a large, skirted vanity dresser with a big square mirror, the kind of dresser where the likes of Marlene Dietrich might sit to do her makeup. Paulita's dresser was covered with cosmetics pots and bottles and had the same sort of fake-ivory brush, comb, mirror, and powder jars that I had seen on my grandmother's dresser. The dresser's mirror was nearly obscured by photos and dance programs stuck into the groove where the glass met the frame.

A round, tufted stool had been pulled up to the vanity, and here Paulita sat, while I sank onto the bed beside Molly. Just above dangled a bare light bulb on its wire. To one side of the dresser I saw a large oval cheval mirror, the kind that stands on the floor in a frame and tilts this way and that. On the floor nearby I saw stacks of photograph albums, little dance-program pencils on strings escaping from between the pages.

On one wall hung a large black and white photo of a flapper, a young woman with huge eyes under a sleek cap of dark hair, eyebrows plucked to the thinnest possible lines. The flapper wore shoes with ankle straps and a costume composed main-ly of a black band around her throat and, beneath spaghetti shoulder straps, row after row of black fringe, ending inch-es above the knee. There were other photos, photos of love-ly but old-fashioned-looking young women, and photos of broad-shouldered men, their mirror-smooth hair shining with brilliantine, in suits with wide lapels and padded shoulders, their shoes gleaming startlingly bright.

Among the photos there were two signed photographs that I remember to this day. One was of Jean Harlow. The plati-num beauty lounged in a white satin gown, looking straight into the camera lens with a kind of smoldering boredom. The other photo was of a silent-movie queen I knew to be Theda Bara. She was dressed as Cleopatra or Mata Hari, or some other Middle-Eastern figure, heavy-lidded in shadowy eye makeup and wearing an Arabian Nights dress that seemed to be more jewelry than clothing.

"Look," Paulita said, stabbing at the signatures with a red fingernail. Both said, "To Paulita," with the star's name signed after. "Look," she said again, "I knew these girls. We were all in the chorus together once." Paulita named a show I didn't recognize. I wondered at the time if she had signed the photos herself.

She pointed to a photo of two suited men with shining hair. "They knew me, too," Paulita said. "They used to take me out all the time." She told us their names, but I didn't know them. "Big producers, they were," she went on. "And they wanted me in their shows."

Paulita snatched a photo album from the floor, opened it, and placed it on the bed. Two photos, mounted on opposite black pages by means of little black paper corners, looked up at Molly and me. They were both of the same young woman, a girl with creamy pale skin, high cheekbones, large eyes, a patrician nose, and a thin blade of chin. She wore a cameo at her throat, white patent high heels, and two fans of white ostrich feathers, strategically positioned. "That's me," she giggled. "I was born beautiful, a dancer. Everyone thought I was as good as any of the stars. But I didn't get the breaks. I just didn't get the breaks. In show business, you have to have the breaks."

I wondered what "the breaks" were. I met Molly's eyes in the gloom. She shrugged and smiled.

On another wall of the cabin I could see clothing hanging on a rope stretched between two spikes nailed into opposite walls. Tarnished sequins glittered, draggled plumes trailed to the floor. An embroidered sleeve of black velvet hung over the back of a straight wooden chair as if resting a languid wrist there. Much of the clothing was black or white, as if from an old-time movie.

From the same photo album, Paulita pulled a dance program. Its miniature pencil dangled at the end of a twisted string. "What is that?" Molly asked. Paulita passed the tiny booklet into Molly's hands and we looked at it together.

"Why, that's a dance program," Paulita said in astonishment.

105

"Don't tell me you have never seen a dance program!"

"I've never seen one," Molly answered, wide-eyed.

"My mother has some in her high school album," I said. "When you got to the dance, they would give you a little book like this one, with a pencil attached by a string, and a tassel. The boy would sign his name in your program for the dances he wanted with you. The little books have numbered lines, one for each dance of the night. That way you could have your whole night filled out, if you were popular. And, Mom says, you can look at them later and remember always."

"That's right," said Paulita with a gleam in her eye. "You can remember always. I used to go to lots of balls. You know what balls are, don't you, girls?"

"Sure," I said. "Cinderella. Gone with the Wind."

Paulita cackled, and I shivered even in the warmth from the stove. From the rope clothesline, she pulled a white dress with a deep v-neck and sparkling rhinestone flowers on each shoulder. "Would you like to try on some of my ball gowns?" She held out the dress to me and I took it from her hands. It smelled old and stale, like sick perfume. Suddenly I felt too closed in, almost suffocated.

"Sorry, but I have to go," I said as politely as I could, passing the gown to Molly. "I told Mother I would be home by now." In truth, I was free to spend the whole day as I liked. But I felt that it was time for me to go.

Without waiting for anyone to say anything, I stepped out into the open air and walked away fast, while I took deep breaths. The sunshine had gone, and a fast-flowing ceiling of clouds, low enough to hide the top of Dollar Mountain, covered the sky.

Goosebumps prickled along my arms with the chill of the fresh wind, and on one ridge of Bald Mountain, a curtain of gray rain was falling. I could smell it in the air; the rain was sweeping down toward town even as I watched.

If I hurried, I could get home before the rain reached the Fourhills.

Striding through the flower meadow, I crossed the dirt road above Mrs. Spiegel's house and broke into a trot. I could smell the rain strongly now, even through the heavy honey of the bitterbrush. As I topped the shoulder of Jagged's lower slope, I turned for a final look at Paulita's cabin.

The plume of smoke from her chimney had flattened, now curling down the roof to the eaves, and the windows looked dark. I didn't see anyone. Molly must still be inside.

I turned downhill, jumped the mossy rivulet, and ran the final hundred yards home.

Just before I reached our yard, the first fat drops of rain smacked into my neck and shoulders. With a final spurt of speed, I reached our steps and pulled open the front door.

Hard rain drummed on the roof and slashed against the windows. I dove into my bedroom and pulled on a soft sweater. From under my bed, I took the narrow black steel box of Prang watercolors with its two little brushes and hard cakes of bright, dry paint.

I found a pencil and a few sheets of typing paper in the kitchen desk. At the sink, I filled a glass with water and laid down my supplies on the yellow Formica table. The rain blurred the view of Dollar from the front window, but that was all right.

I was ready to paint.

As I sat at the kitchen table, I remembered the flowers. Sliding two fingers into my right jeans pocket, I touched something limp and cool. With great care I drew out two crumpled flowers and a handful of bruised and folded leaves with broken stalks. Against the strong yellow of the Formica tabletop, the violets looked pale and lifeless. The maroon on the undersides of the leaves showed the color of old blood. Still, they were beautiful.

I took up the pencil and did my best to sketch the violets. Presently the front door opened and Mother carried two rain-spotted brown paper grocery bags into the kitchen and set them down on the linoleum countertop. Bustling about as she put things away, Mom looked over my shoulder now and then as I painted.

Finally, she said quietly, "It isn't going very well this time, is it?"

"No," I said, after a long pause. "I went to Paulita's today," I continued. "Molly was in her cabin and they invited me in."

I sensed in Mother a kind of heightened alertness, but she said only, "Was it interesting?"

"Yes," I said slowly. "It was interesting. Paulita has pictures of when she was young and a lot of pretty dresses and a very nice mirror and a good wood stove. She used to be a dancer and was in the silent movies." I put down my pencil. The drawing was not going well. I would have to start over on a clean piece of paper; it would not do to waste the flowers.

"It's dark in her cabin, Mom," I tried to explain. "Everything there is in the past. I like the past, and I like the dark. But there's a shadow."

Mom nodded and opened the refrigerator to put the milk away. "Yes," she said. She smiled.

New Stars at Little Falls

Dad was a prospector. He taught himself structural geology and a good bit of mineralogy, both from books and by offering to guide geologists sent out by mining companies to do mineral exploration in the mountains around us.

After spending a weekend guiding a geologist from Anaconda Corporation, Dad told us, "I can do what that guy is doing now; I know about contact zones, about stoping, how metamorphism works, how crystals form, how to send rocks off for assay—and I'm going to find us a mine!" Before long, a corner of our basement had been set up with a Bunsen burner, flasks, vials, eyedroppers of acid, hardness tables, and a stack of claim location papers next to a shoebox of empty Prince Albert tobacco cans. We got a Geiger counter, and then a black-light. Dad was going for it.

Considering that his prospecting activities occurred only in summer evenings and on his days off (and it was rare for him to have an entire weekend off in the summer), what he achieved amazes me still. During the long Idaho summer twilights, on nights when we didn't fly fish, Dad would load us into our little red Jeep, the top off, of course (the better to see rock outcroppings in the mountains), and we would head up one of the many dirt roads to explore.

When Dad saw a promising rock outcrop, he'd stop the Jeep, jump out, and hike straight up to it, rock-hammer out

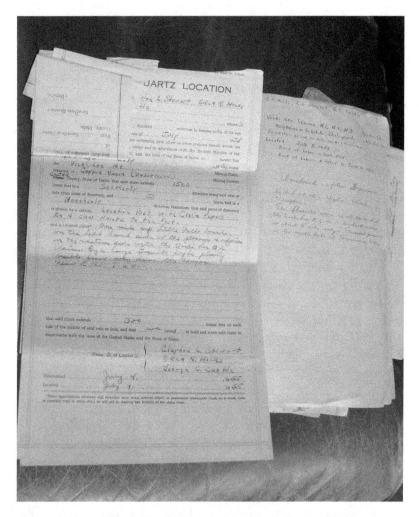

Dad's prospecting ledger, with maps, claim papers, and stories of lost mines from old-timers. This is the description of the Vicki Lee claim (named after my sister) that Dad found up Little Falls Creek.

and swinging. He'd come running zigzag down to the Jeep, holding out a rock specimen, and would say to my mom, "Look, Bernice, just as I thought—that outcrop wasn't quartz, it's gray feldspar. Orthoclase. But there aren't any inclusions, even at the contact." My sister, small Vicki, and I would peer over Mom's shoulder at the rock. I'd smile. If the rock didn't have any inclusions of some precious mineral, Dad wouldn't want to keep it, so I would have another specimen for my rock collection.

Some minerals were easy to identify, even for a child of twelve. We learned to pan for gold, and found it, too, adding the bright grains to vials that Dad kept in a glass case on the bedroom wall. Iron pyrite, "fools' gold," though without commercial value, was beautifully identifiable. The copper minerals, azurite and malachite, announced themselves with their signature colors of bright blue and bright green. And galena, with its chunky metallic sheen, was unmistakable. Other minerals were not easy to spot, even when seen in bright sunlight. But some of these elusive minerals would reveal themselves under a blacklight.

In 1958, the Fourth of July fell on a Friday. Mom told Vicki and me to be home from our summer kid doings by three in the afternoon so we could help her pack for a camping trip. "We're going over Trail Creek Summit as soon as your dad gets off work," she said. "He got tomorrow off! We'll camp somewhere along Summit Creek, and we can fish tomorrow. He's taking the blacklight this time, and tonight he said we're going up Little Falls Creek to look for something special."

"Do you know what it is?" I asked, incurably curious.

"Tungsten," she pronounced. "It's a metal they use in making light bulbs. There's a name for the ore he's looking for, but I don't remember. You can ask him."

"Tungsten," I whispered to myself. I had heard at school that the glowing filaments inside light bulbs were made of tungsten.

The word sounded very important and official. Every house, every store, even cars had light bulbs. And yet, we were going to look for tungsten up a narrow, steep canyon with no homes, on a road that could only be navigated by a Jeep, where there was no electricity—and had never been any—except for summer lightning and perhaps some lonely hunter's flashlight.

After I had helped Mom and Vicki load food, sleeping bags, some other bits (jackets, fishing gear and our tent into the Jeep, I ran downstairs and brought up four Prince Albert tobacco cans, a hammer and some shingle nails, and a small stack of claim forms. You never knew!

Dad got home about six. He added a rock-hammer and the blacklight to the Jeep, changed clothes, and we were off. We didn't pass a single car on the way over Trail Creek Summit —a good thing, because there weren't many places where two vehicles could pass. Along Summit Creek, no one was camped in the willow meadows—indeed, we saw no one camped at all. "I imagine that everybody went to Hailey for the fireworks," Mom said. "Or, if someone is up here, they went on down to Wildhorse Creek or the East Fork of the Lost, where there's bigger water and bigger fish."

Two hours later the tent was up, the sleeping bags unrolled, the hot dogs and potato salad eaten, and the coffee pot empty. The cooking fire was doused, and we were ready to go. Dad said that the three of us would have to stay near the bottom of the hill so we didn't fall in the rocks, while he would take the blacklight and climb straight up a certain talus slope. "There's a gray outcrop above that talus, Danny," he told me as we were cleaning up the campsite after dinner. "I've looked at it with the binoculars. And for hundreds or even thousands of years, that talus has been breaking off that cliff near the top of the ridge and rolling down the slope. When minerals roll down a slope away from where they were to start with, we call that stuff 'float.' If the mineral shows up in a blacklight, you can use the blacklight to follow the float all the way uphill to where it came from. And then you can stake your claim."

"Tungsten," I said. "Mom told me you think there is tungsten up Little Falls."

"Weeell," he said slowly, dragging a hand down his jaw. "Maybe. I hope so. It's highly metamorphic up there. Everything is all twisted and melted and squashed, and the rock types are right. There's only one way to find out. Come on, let's hurry."

We had been exploring up Little Falls Creek before—the narrow little canyon was an explosion of rock outcrops, little cliffs, long gray and red talus slopes, and huge boulders, with scattered pines and an ice-clear creek at the bottom. And we had explored in many canyons until long after dark before heading home. But going up a canyon on a steep, treacherous road in the dark? That was new. I held onto the fender bar on my side of the Jeep with a death grip. This would be an adventure.

Little Falls canyon was silent and as dark as black velvet. The Milky Way arched above, as brilliant with stars as only a sky can be at high altitude. The Jeep slowed to a crawl as we started up the slope. Dad reached down and put it into 4x4 low. The blacklight's wooden box bumped my legs as Dad negotiated the Jeep over large rocks. I tried not to think of the 100-foot drop on the downhill side of the road, a drop that soon became a 200-foot drop. I could smell the pines and hear the rushing of the little creek far below, tumbling over angular boulders. The night was still; not a bird cried, not a breath of wind stirred.

After less than a mile, Dad stopped the Jeep and pulled on the brake. "Here we are," he said to Mom. "I mileaged it out last time so I could mileage it back in, in the dark. Can't turn the Jeep around here, so I'm going to have to back all the way down when we leave. You'll have to walk ahead of me with the flashlight then." Mom nodded. She was used to such doings.

"OK," Dad said, unfolding his long legs to stand on the road, which was nothing but a somewhat flat trail in the tumbled rocks—no dirt was in sight. "We'll go together down to the creek and cross over. You three can stay by the creek. I'll go on up the other side a bit. Then the flashlight goes off and I turn on the blacklight and start looking for float."

I remembered that tungsten ore had a name. "What's the ore called?" I asked.

"It's called scheelite," he said, "and if it's here, if you see it, you'll know it.

Scheelite fluoresces blue—bright light blue. I've seen pictures of it. But don't get your hopes up too high. Chances are there won't be any."

Slowly and we climbed down through the sharp talus to the creek and crossed on a fallen log. With just her flashlight to lead us down through the broken rock, Mom kept us girls close to her, especially six-year-old Vicki. The looming east ridge and its train of talus seemed blacker than coal. The cliff high above was invisible, a dark mass that cut off the sky full of stars.

"Scheelite," I thought. I had never heard the word before, and it sounded like something a troll would have. "Scheelite," I thought, trying to make it into a story. "And in the far reaches of his cave, the troll's treasure lay heaped nearly to the roof— gold and rubies and scheelite."

"OK, Bernice," Dad called; by this time he was fifty yards further up the slope. "No more flashlight. I'm turning on the blacklight. You girls had better stay there." Mother and Vicki found flat rocks and sat, but despite the darkness, I began to climb after Dad, feeling my way on all fours so I wouldn't fall.

I could hear his feet above me, sliding along the rocks, and was careful not to place myself immediately below. The only sounds were feet on rocks and the faint sigh of Little Falls Creek, now lost in the darkness below. I knew Dad knew I was there, and he slowed a little until I was nearly even with him on the slope.

Just as I was beginning to feel tired, I heard Dad stop about five feet above me and a little to the west. "Just look, Danny," he said, and I could see the sweep of his arm as a change in the blackness against the sky. "Look at all the stars."

I climbed even with him. "There's Cassie's chair," I said.

Dad had taught me some of the constellations. "And look, there's the Big Dipper and the pointer stars, and there's my favorite, the North Star," he said. "Do you remember its other name?"

"Polaris," I said in a hushed whisper. The stars were so many and so bright that the constellations we saw from home every night seemed overwhelmed. We stood staring into the depths of the sky for a long moment.

"Well, here goes," I heard Dad mutter. He switched on the blacklight.

The stars! The stars! The Milky Way and all her cohort blazed overhead, but around our feet, up the ridge, *far* up the ridge— all around us, fading to pinpoints in the distance—shone a galaxy of bright blue stars.

Abruptly, Dad sat down in the rocks, and the blue stars shifted as the blacklight moved with him.

"Scheelite," he whispered. "It's here. I found it."

As he sat in the rocks, a glowing piece of scheelite in his hand, the waning moon crested the cliff and washed Little Falls Creek canyon in cold white light. But the moon came too late. He had found the stars.

Seven and Two

In 1952, MGM was filming the musical *Seven Brides for Seven Brothers*, a song-and-dance romp starring Jane Powell, Howard Keel, and Russ Tamblyn. The plot: seven brothers are living way at the back of beyond, up a narrow canyon. The oldest brother marries a young woman from the closest town. In that town live six unmarried young women, but bachelors are few. The six younger brothers kidnap the six women, take them to their home, and then SMASH! An avalanche thunders tons of snow across the mouth of the canyon, sealing them all inside until spring snowmelt. There are protests and mild dust-ups, but by spring, there are seven couples eager for lives of domestic bliss.

As the movie contact man for Sun Valley (one of his many hats), Dad met with the director, Stanley Donen. MGM had come to Sun Valley because *Seven Brides* needed an avalanche.

By the time the film crew came to Sun Valley, much of the indoor filming of *Seven Brides* had been completed. The only outdoor scenes remaining were a scene with the actors heading toward the narrows in the snow, and the avalanche itself. It became Dad's task to find a place that would work. Once he found that place, he would have to get the US Forest Service to allow MGM to set dynamite charges for the tumbling fall of snow. Fortunately, that was a very snowy year at Sun Valley.

Dad found a place. Northeast of Sun Valley, a dirt road twists steeply up the side of Trail Creek Canyon, topping out at 7,800 feet and continuing on toward Big Lost River. This road was not (and to this day is not) plowed in winter. From Sun Valley, the road was plowed for only a mile, to Trail Creek Cabin, a cozy place where catered parties and sleighrides could be arranged.

But several miles farther up Trail Creek Road, Dad knew, lay a steep and narrow side canyon, Corral Creek Canyon. He took a snowcat to investigate (of course, there were no snowmobiles in those days). Yes, Corral Creek Canyon would be perfect, the film crew agreed when he returned with them the following day. The Forest Service was happy, too.

Dad sent his snowplows to Trail Creek Cabin to begin plowing. In two days, the plows had opened the snow-closed road six miles farther north, at which point Dad had the plows turn off the main route and continue on up Corral Creek. In a snow-covered meadow before the canyon narrowed, Dad had them plow out a large parking lot for the movie vehicles and equipment. A narrow road was plowed from this parking lot farther up the canyon, ending in a very small parking lot just large enough for the snowplows to turn around: the staging area from which the crew could set the dynamite charges. They would string a long wire back to the main parking lot and do the actual filming there.

Their work done, the snowplows headed back to the Sun Valley garage.

Dad surveyed the scene with the film crew that afternoon. Yes, Corral Creek Canyon would work well; everyone was satisfied.

The following day, the newly plowed six miles hummed with traffic, from Trail Creek Cabin to Corral Creek, for the first time in months. Trucks and cars bore people, cameras, tripods, lights, generators, wooden platforms, and enough tables, chairs, and food for all the participants. There was a great bustle in the parking lot as equipment setup began.

Lights were plugged into generators, chairs were unfolded, and the director and his assistants walked slowly here and there, planning the shoot.

Urns of coffee and rows of cups were set out on the tables, and people cheerfully held the steaming mugs to warm their hands. It was cold. Every night for the past week had been colder than 20 degrees below zero, and the days were freezing as well.

The setup and dry run went well. I was seven years old that winter, and even so have kept a clear, sunny memory of Russ Tamblyn striding across a parking lot back at Sun Valley, his parka bright against the white and piled snow. Dad came home red-faced from the cold but enthusiastic. Everything was working. Everything was going to be perfect.

Everything was perfect.

The day of the shoot dawned clear and windless, the sunlight flooding down the smooth white slopes into the bottom of Trail Creek Canyon. Trucks and cars rolled early on the white road to Corral Creek.

The dynamite charges were set and the cameras positioned. There would be only four hours of sunlight in Corral Creek Canyon before the sun would wink out on the west ridge of Trail Creek Canyon. And in snow, there are no do-overs. Things have to be right the first time, because there are tracks.

The actors played their scene in the pristine snow, cameras rolling in the cold. That went well. They returned to the parking lot for food and coffee.

With time to spare, everything was made ready for the avalanche. The dynamite was placed, the long wire strung out, and the people and vehicles abandoned the little turnaround parking lot and crouched behind trucks and trailers. Finally, the director called "Action," and BOOM!

The side of the canyon seemed to jump with shock, then broke and swept down to the bottom of the canyon. Snow forty feet deep smothered the end of the road extension where Dad's snowplows had turned around. Captured forever on film was the avalanche, exactly what was needed for *Seven Brides for Seven Brothers*. Everyone went back to Sun Valley satisfied and full of strong coffee.

The MGM film crew left Sun Valley. The six-mile road from Trail Creek Cabin to Corral Creek snowed and drifted shut. In the spring, the piled snow from the avalanche eventually melted and flowed into Corral Creek, from there into Trail Creek, and was gone.

Seven Brides for Seven Brothers was released into theatres, and the movie was a hit. We watched it at the Sun Valley Opera House, and Dad whispered, "Look, there it is! There's the avalanche I helped set up. Gee, it looks small on film, doesn't it?" He rubbed at his jaw and shook his head. "All that work for just a few seconds."

Seven Brides passed from the theatre, and years passed in Corral Creek Canyon. Summers came and went. Aspens greened up, turned gold, and dropped their leaves. Winters snowed and melted. I was now a teenager, thirteen years old. There had been no more avalanches up Corral Creek Canyon.

At school, one of my friends was Thelma, a lively girl in my class at Ketchum Grade School. Thelma had two older brothers, Billy and Russell. Billy and Russell went deer hunting that fall. With their rifles, they walked up Corral Creek Canyon.

What they found was not a deer, but a skull, a human skull.

Billy and Russell took the skull to the sheriff. At school that fall, we all thought Billy and Russell were extremely cool, because the sheriff and his deputies went back up Corral Creek Canyon and found another skull, plus the widely scattered and fragmented bones of two men, with various remnants of their clothing—zippers, bits of cloth, curled-up shoes, buttons. Oddly, these bits were as scattered as the bones.

The sheriff had dental records checked, and after some time

he learned that the skulls belonged to two convicts who had escaped from the Utah State Penitentiary one freezing winter night years before. "Probably on their way to Canada," townspeople speculated. "The road over Trail Creek Summit would look open on a map. Poor guys. How could they have known that the road is never plowed in the winter? They must have tried to get through and froze to death. Wild animals must have scattered the bones."

But that winter was different. That winter, the road over Trail Creek Summit was plowed for six miles. For several days, there were crisp new tire tracks on that road. And why would they have turned from the main canyon to Corral Creek Canyon, so pinched and narrow, heading almost straight east into the Pioneer Range?

It was Dad who put it together for us. The Utah convicts had escaped only days before the filming of the avalanche. Dad figured that the two men were indeed headed for Canada. Their most direct route would take them north from Utah to Sun Valley, and the most direct route to Canada would appear to be the Trail Creek Road, if all you had for a guide was a map. Dad told us that he thought the men hitchhiked to Sun Valley and continued north from Trail Creek Cabin on foot, hoping to catch another ride, or even to stop someone and take a car, walking the six miles of plowed road and expecting it to continue on to the Big Lost country. They wouldn't realize that the detour up Corral Creek was not the main road. And the fresh tire tracks would show even in moonlight.

But, of course, no cars and trucks came, and eventually the escapees reached the end of the road and wondered what to do as the last of the light faded. Perhaps they spent a very chilly night huddled near the equipment trailers in the new parking lot.

With the morning sunlight would come a convoy of movie makers. Dad reasoned that when the movie people began arriving, the convicts retreated up the narrow road extension to hide behind piled snow in the place where the snowplows turned around, perhaps planning to come out and walk back to Sun Valley after dark.

And then, *BOOM!* The avalanche buried them forty feet deep in snow, rending them limb from limb, scattering their clothing and their bones. No one would find them until years later, when Billy and Russell decided to go deer hunting.

The Horned Skull

I was fourteen years old, school was out for the summer, and I was about to have a perfect day.

For the past few days I had been staying with family friends George and Annette Castle, at their lumber camp up Peach Creek, a small tributary of the Salmon River. I helped Annette with meals for the logging crew, so usually our days were made up of short outings punctuated by duty, but this day was special—a day off for the crew. George had driven his pickup into Challis to pick up needed parts. Annette and I had the Cadillac, a great, green, monstery gas-slurping dinosaur that was surprisingly rugged on tiny back roads, especially since Annette thought that getting places was more important than avoiding dents and scratches. We had with us a picnic lunch, soda pop in the cooler, day packs, rock hammers, and a good idea.

Annette and I were rock hounds, one of the reasons a fast friendship between a young girl and a middle-aged woman had begun and flourished.

Today we were on the hunt for amethyst geodes, and Annette had a possible place in mind. It was June, with a sky full of blue-bottomed puffy clouds and a valley floor full of moving cloud shadows.

Leaving clouds of dust, we swooped down the hairpin turns of the Peach Creek road and drove along the Salmon River, curving and curving until we came to the valley of the Lost River, a long east-west valley where we planned to look for our rock-hunting place.

Sunlight sparkled on the river. I remember seeing a female merganser with her brood of tiny ducklings hopping on and off her back as they drifted along on the current, in and out of cottonwood shadows. Everything was green and growing, and the world smelled fresh and new. We had all the windows in the big green-and-cream Cadillac rolled all the way down, and the world was good.

We turned east toward the Lost River country just before the small town of Challis, and drove for some time.

Eventually Annette said, "Start looking on the right for a little road, a little dirt road with a gate in the fence at the highway."

Clutching the window ledge, I leaned my head out into the fresh wind. There it was, a road so small that it showed as two dirt tracks with sagebrush and grasses growing down the center.

We turned off the state highway and opened the barbed-wire gate. When I got back into the Cadillac, I could detect the faint perfume of the fried chicken we had made early that morning. Annette was smiling a little smile.

We slid through a wet meadow with countless buttercup-faces looking up through the dark sedge where a few cattle were grazing, and then we bumped across a sagebrush flat starred with pink phlox, bluebells, and yellow violets.

The road lifted, and we drove up into a system of dry hills, foothills of unnamed mountains, pricked here and there with the exclamation points of scarlet Indian paintbrush.

Once in the hills, we began to see rock outcrops of various sorts, and Annette squinted out the window and slowed the Cadillac, looking thoughtful.

After a few more miles, we crested yet another little ridge, and there before us was an outcrop of broken reddish rock just down from the hilltop, with rock spoil spilling all the way down the hill into the grass at the bottom of a draw. "I think this must be it," Annette said, and the Cadillac lurched to a stop.

We grabbed our rock hammers and jumped out into the sunshine.

I looked back toward the highway and was surprised at how high we were now. The cattle in the wet meadow didn't look like ants, but they were definitely very small cows! Trucks on the highway were barely to be seen, big semis looking like tiny pale boxes crawling on a long, gray thread.

Annette and I were alone with the day, and ready for anything.

We turned our attention to the rock outcrop. We knew that amethyst crystals occurred in Idaho but were rare here. Amethyst was my favorite gem, and I was and am in love with native crystals, a love that preceded the new-agers by several decades.

The clouds grew sparse, the sun beat down upon our necks, and Annette jammed on her trademark wide-brimmed straw hat and donned her pale blue rock-hunting gloves. We walked down the hillside along the rock outcrop for a hundred yards, and suddenly Annette reached down and lifted a fist-sized stone. "Look," she said in triumph. "This is the right place. This is a geode!"

We were thrilled. I had seen many geodes in collections, those lovely stone eggs of agate that are sometimes hollow and lined with beautiful crystals, but I had never found one myself.

Annette steadied the geode on a larger rock and struck it with her hammer, a light but sharp blow. The geode broke cleanly into two pieces, 2/3–1/3. Annette was very good with a rock hammer. The thing was hollow, and the tablespoon-sized cavity within was lined with small crystals. The crystals were clear quartz, not purple, but nevertheless were very exciting indeed.

We worked our way down the hill for what seemed a time-less while, picking up broken geodes and stowing some intact geodes away in our packs for later surprises, since both Annette and my father had rock saws.

Then Annette cracked another one and said, "Look, ame-thyst!" I scrambled across a loose-dirt slope to get to her.

Sure enough, the crystals inside were purple—well, they weren't *purple* purple, they were lilac. But we had found amethysts! We looked at each other in that breathless silence that comes with discovery. We had found them!

Suddenly I realized that we were no longer alone. Several inquisitive faces peered down at us from the crest of the hill. After a startled moment, I realized that our visitors were ante-lope.

Annette had a way with animals, the like of which I have never seen. In years to come, I would see a number of wild animals approach Annette to have ticks or thorns removed or to take a treat from her hand, but this was the first time.

She said, "Let's have them come down to us," and sat herself in the dirt. I did the same, and when Annette began to wave her rock hammer gently from side to side, I waved mine, too.

Three big-eyed does came slowly over the crest of the hill, each followed by a tiny, long-legged fawn. They came silently, with necks extended and nostrils wide and sniffing. As Annette waved her hammer, she began to hum a little tune, and still they came. In awe I watched the antelope come closer and clos-er, until I could count their eyelashes and see beads of moisture on the patent-leather noses of the little fawns.

One doe walked right up to Annette. I noticed that this doe had several ticks on her face just below one eye. Still hum-ming, Annette laid her hammer in the dirt and pulled off her gloves. I expected the does to spook at any moment, but the others stood still on the soft dirt of the hillside and waited while Annette removed several ticks from the doe that had come to

125

her.

Then, far below us down the hill, I heard a snort. A large buck antelope stood for a moment at the bottom of the draw and then bolted east across the toe of the slope. All three does, as well as the fawns, jerked their heads up abruptly and followed him, half-galloping, half-sliding down the loose dirt and rocks until they reached the bottom of the draw, then continuing east at full gallop until they topped the next ridge. There, one of the does stopped to look at us over her shoulder. Then they were gone, a slight flavor of dust in the air the only evidence that the antelope had been there at all.

I put my hand flat on the ground to help myself up, and through the dirt I felt them running, drumming on the soil somewhere over the next ridge, diminishing. They were gone.

Annette and I climbed back to the Cadillac and spread a blanket. We laid out the fried chicken, macaroni salad, and long green onions, and set forth two bottles of cold orange pop from the cooler. Meadowlarks sang all around, and a mountain bluebird sat on a sagebrush and looked at us for a moment. We ate our food rapidly, eager to get back to the finding.

Then we slid back down the hill to the place of the amethyst geodes, and searched away the afternoon under the warm early-summer sun at 5,000 feet. I found some amethyst myself, Annette found more, and we were already counting our day a great success.

I slid still lower on the hill and found more geodes, including some very lovely banded-agate geodes already broken open. I had to have them, and pictured the look on Mother's face when I showed them to her.

Then, as well as the agates, I began to find bones.

At fourteen, I didn't know very much about bones. But I knew that these bones were from an animal at least as large as a sheep, and that some were vertebrae and most of them were ribs. The bones were glossy, stained a bright rust color to match the soil where they lay. I hefted a rib bone and tapped it gently against my front teeth, and I felt the sharp and glassy sensation of rock. This was not a real bone, but a fossil!

I gathered a few of the bones, then looked at my pack. Already my pack was bulging. Any more rocks and I wouldn't be able to carry it up the hill, and anyway, there was no room left for the fossils.

"We'll be coming back," I thought. "This place is easy to find. I'll get the bones then."

I stood up and shouldered the pack. It was so heavy I could barely stand. "Why, it's late," I thought. The sun was only a finger's width from the western mountains, and gray clouds were flying toward us from the south. I looked for Annette and found her on the slope above me. She was already climbing toward the car. She knew she didn't need to call me. I began the long, slow climb with the heavy pack.

Then I saw something I had not noticed before. There in a jumble of rocks sat a delicate little skull, a skull smaller than my fist. The skull was not rust-red, hard, and shiny like the fossils, but chalky white and light to the touch like real bone that had been exposed to sun and rain. It came easily from the rock pile.

The empty eye sockets stared at me as I turned the skull in my hands. Then the flying clouds overhead seemed to stop stock-still in the air. Even the breeze held its breath. With a little rush, my brain caught up with my eyes and hands. What *was* this skull?

I had thought, "Baby antelope." *Wait,* the brain said as the world began to move once more. *Antelope fawns don't have horns. And this skull has horns.*

This was not the skull of a newborn antelope, nor was it the skull of a deer or an elk fawn. I knew that such fawns aren't born with antlers. Nevertheless, the small skull had horns. From the flat of the skull in front of the eyes rose a structure of forked bone rather like a gun sight. I noticed that the teeth were like the teeth of a ground squirrel or a beaver.

I had become disoriented and swayed dizzily in my tracks. I remembered to put my foot down and stood motionless while the sky seemed to darken.

The four-inch skull smiled its white smile in the fading sunlight. I shivered. The thing was real, but it was alien, a thing outside my experience, outside my reading, outside everything I knew.

With great care, I set the small skull on a flat rock and stepped away. This was a thing I could not fathom, and I said to myself, knowing that I was rationalizing, "We'll come back later in the summer, when I don't have a pack full of rocks. If I try to take this now, I will fall and crush it. I can find it again." I left the horned skull on the rock and toiled up the hill after Annette.

Once I looked back. The skull remained, a white blotch in the rust-red of rock and soil. I topped the hill, slung my pack into the trunk of the Cadillac, and collapsed wearily into the passenger seat.

"Let's be off," said Annette jauntily. "It's been a great day!"

"We'll come back here, won't we?" I asked. I tried not to look over my shoulder.

"Of course we'll come back," she said, turning the key.

We bounced happily down and out of the hills. Stacked bars of golden cloud toward the west began to put together a memorable sunset. I thought of my amethyst geodes with a smile. Wait until Mom and Dad see these! And I thought of the little skull now alone on the hillside once more, pale in the fading light. Of course, I would come back for it. And in some way the thing would become comprehensible, would be made a part of the way the world operates and the way things can be explained.

The sun sank, we pulled out onto the Challis highway, and the day became a memory that has lasted for more than sixty years.

We never went back to the geode place. For years, on the rare occasions when the family drove past those foothills, I would watch for the little road across the meadow with the barbed-wire gate. No one ever wanted to go up into the rust-red foothills but me; we always seemed to be in a hurry when we drove the Challis highway, and I didn't go back.

When I was twenty, one bright June day I drove my own first car over Galena Summit and continued for hours down the Salmon River canyon until I turned east from Challis and began to search for the little road, the gate, the small meadow, and the red foothills, but nothing was the same. I drove for many miles in that valley, and found no gate in the long line of fence. No little meadow on the flats was to be seen, and the foothills did not look at all like those in my memory. I couldn't find the geode place.

Later, much later, I learned of the prairie-dog-like mylagaulid rodents of the ancient past, long-clawed burrowing fellows, each with an elevated fork of bone on the skull in front of the eyes. Mylagaulids have been extinct for tens of thousands of years. No fossil mylagaulids have ever been found in Idaho. Remembering the skull I left behind, I consulted maps of the geology of that area. The rock layers in that part of central Idaho are relatively new. No mylagaulid fossils have ever been found in layers as recent as those of the red foothills in that country.

I have searched again, several times, but I have never found the geode place, and I have not seen the horned skull again. Annette cannot take me there, for she has gone to the unknown hills where I cannot yet follow.

Was the skull just a small and shivery grace note placed by Providence into a perfect day so that I would not excite the envy of the gods? I don't think so. I think that to this day the horned skull waits for me on a flat rock, eye sockets cobwebbed over, sharp teeth now loose in chalky sockets, tiny horns casting pointed shadows on the red soil of the hillside. Is it the fossil skull of a long-extinct mylogaulid rodent, a skull of stone? Or, perhaps, did a lost colony of horned prairie dogs survive until recent times, isolated in those phantom red hills?

An Afternoon in Gramps' Waders

I was fourteen and had my daytime driver's license. This meant freedom for me—and at fourteen and in midsummer, for me freedom simply meant freedom to fly fish.

During my high school years, my summer job was tending to the golf carts at the Sun Valley resort's golf course. When the carts came in at the end of the day, I would gather and throw away all the candy bar wrappers, potato chip bags, empty bourbon bottles, beer cans, and gobs of chewing gum, wipe down the seats, and plug each cart into its charger overnight. Eventually, I learned to do small repairs as well, and was inordinately proud when I could say to myself in tones reminiscent of Tom, the valley's master mechanic, "Yup. It's a bad solenoid. Better get rid of that bad 'un and put a new 'un in. Then she'll be AOK." Of course, when a real problem arose, I left a note on the bad cart for Tom, who would take care of it the next morning.

This was an ideal job for a solitary teenage dreamer like me. Though tending the golf carts took only two to four hours a day, I was making as much money as most of my classmates who worked 40-hour weeks every summer. I made a hundred and twenty dollars a month!

On this hot August day, I was driving Gramps' 1948 half-ton pickup, a big snub-nosed fellow named the Express, and I was going north. The Express had been bought new by Sun

Valley Company when Sun Valley was still part of the Utah Parks division of Union Pacific Railroad, and for many years it wore the gray and gold livery of UPRR, with the familiar stars-and-stripes shield on the door. Every day, the Express would drive a mile from Sun Valley down to the UPRR depot in Ketchum, not far from the Warm Springs bridge, to pick up tourists' baggage, taking it to the Sun Valley Lodge and the Challenger Inn. There the bags were offloaded and carried by bellboys to the rooms.

Driving the Express, I liked to think of his having carried the baggage of Marilyn Monroe, or Clark Gable, James Arness, Claudette Colbert, Gary Cooper, Barbara Stanwyck, Lucille Ball and Desi Arnaz–the list was almost endless. What if full-length mink coats had ridden in the Express? Perhaps fabulous gowns owned by Marilyn had been slung back there in the wooden bed inside a smooth leather suitcase. Or how about Gary Cooper's shotgun? Or, for that matter, Barbara Stanwyck's shotgun? Maybe they had bounced side by side in fancily tooled cases all the way from the Ketchum train depot to the Challenger Inn.

When Gramps retired from Sun Valley, he "retired" the Express by buying the old pickup when it was no longer needed, and it became his fishing truck.

But today was my day, and today the Express was sober in a new dress of plain tan paint, expertly sprayed onto it by Gramps himself. There was nothing in the pickup bed but my fishing gear and Gramps' old chest waders, and the Express had nothing to do but to take me fishing at the bottom of Trail Creek Summit until it was time to plug in and clean out the golf carts, which I would do on my way home.

I pulled off the dirt road onto the sagebrush bench just beyond the mouth of Corral Creek and stopped the Express. No one else was fishing here yet. These ponds were only a few miles from town and were popular; by evening two or three people would be fishing them, but not now. Early afternoon on a stifling August day was definitely not the best time to fly fish large beaver ponds.

With the current of a stream to help conceal the laydown of the line, yes, it was easy to fly fish and catch trout in the middle of a summer day unless you were an idiot. But getting trout to come to the surface of a great calm mirror and not be spooked by the laying down of the line–*and bite*–now, in the heat of the day—that took finesse. I had come to practice, practice, practice. And who knows? Maybe I could make a few of them bite. I wolfed my bologna sandwich and gulped my bottle of Grape Nehi. Time to get going.

I hopped out of the Express and suddenly it hit me: I had on the wrong shoes! These were my brand-new blue tennis shoes and were going to have to last me for months, if not all through the next school year! I had tried them on first thing in the morning and had forgotten to trade them for my old, holey fishing tennis shoes before leaving home. Oh, no! I walked slowly around to the back of the pickup and looked at my fly rod case. Darn. Mom would really hate it if I got muck all over and inside these new shoes, but the beaver ponds were in a marsh and I knew I couldn't fish them without slogging through sedges and mud. Darn again. I would have to go home, and the day would be spoiled.

Then my eyes lit upon Gramps' old chest waders. I never wore waders, not even when it was cold, always just charging into the water and coming home with wet jeans and wet shoes. But I would wear waders today! They would save my new shoes.

I pulled them on with some difficulty and stood up. The top of the waders was supposed to come up under the armpits, but it rode, baggily, at my waist, because the waders were men's waders and I was five feet two. I moved the toothy metal sliders and tightened the suspenders as tight as they would go. The straps were so shortened that the sliders ended up over my shoulders in the back. But the waders weren't falling down anymore, so that was all right. Feeling like an elephant in the process of shedding its skin, I started down the rock and dirt trail to the first beaver pond. And I fell.

The waders, with their rigid and very much too large gum-shoe boot-bottoms, made me awkward. I picked myself up and went on more carefully. This would be an interesting day. But at least my new shoes would be protected, and the day would be saved.

I got to the first pond, a beautiful oval sky-mirror about 80 feet long and 40 feet wide, set like an opal into a ring of foot-deep sedge. Perfect. The beaver dam across the bottom was old, and so the pond was nearly filled with silt and quite shallow. The snag of a dead cottonwood stood like a spear in the water on the far side of the pond, and the woven sticks of the dam were ancient and white as bones. On the dirt in the dam, mon-keyflower was growing, and sedges, and a clump of stinging nettle. Likely, this pond had few fish, and if there were any, they would be small. But it was an ideal place to limber up my cast.

I fell again clambering up on the old beaver dam to the place where I stood to cast. Wearing waders would take some getting used to.

There was no wind, and I cast my line. It floated through the air straight and true and alighted on the surface of the water as tenderly as the brush of a moth's wing, with scarcely the ghost of a ripple. I would never match Dad's skill, but I was already better than most, and I was going to be good someday. I cast over and over, practicing lifting the long line off the water as softly as I could lay it down. It felt good. Across the pond, a long stem of yarrow, topped by its flat white flower, leaned low from the bank over the water. I aimed my cast and laid out the line so that the fly came to rest dangling an inch over the yarrow. A small pull of the line and the fly popped over the yarrow stem and fell onto the water just as if it had been a living insect. A

134

bump came from below and I tugged sharply. I had one on.

The trout came easily to my hand as I reeled in, a little brookie, only a fingerling but fighting as hard as it was able. I released the small one and it dived into the loose algae and silt in the water at my feet and disappeared. I rinsed the fly and corralled my line. Time to move on. If they would actually bite now, I should be at a pond with larger fish.

Sloshing ponderously through the mud and sedges of the meadow between ponds, I found I could no longer jump the narrow, deeply cut, and many-channeled small stream that wound its way through the wet meadows among the beaver ponds, but had to climb down into each channel and pull myself laboriously up onto the opposite bank every time I crossed. Wearing waders was not fun.

I followed the current upstream and came to the foot of a large, active beaver dam some eight feet high. The bottom layer of this dam was old, with white, barkless branches and a growth of new willow shoots in the soil between them. But the upper tier of the dam was new. No plants had taken root here. The twigs and mud mortar still had a raw, fresh look to them, with smooth bark on the twigs and even a few withering leaves on branchlets here and there. In the center of the dam, the rim was punctuated by a small rivulet of water pouring over the new weave of green twigs and mud. All along the top of the dam the mud was still wet, and a branch with bright green leaves stuck out at an odd angle.

I began to climb up the dam. It was quite a tall dam; this pond would probably be deep enough for keepable fish. Hand over hand I pulled myself to the rim and looked out over the water. A resounding *slap!* told me what I had figured already; this was an active beaver pond. A furry brown head arrowed through the pond away from me, and farther to the west, two more beavers, smaller, swam away. Over to the northwest was their lodge, a hump bristling with young willows. The little pair of beavers made for that and disappeared, but the larger beaver slowed and stopped, clinging to a half-submerged log some distance away.

I looked down into the water. This pond had the fluffy silt bottom of an old pond, but the new buildup on the old dam made it deep. There would be good fish here.

Balanced on the rim of the dam, I cast out toward a pair of shaving-brush willow trees near the opposite bank, many-trunked, squatty, and with their feet in the water. There was a deep shadow under their branches, and if I could land my fly there without catching it on the drooping twigs, I might wake up a sleeping trout.

I cast and the fly landed in the center of the shadow. Something rocketed through the surface and jumped. A miss! But that trout was awake now. I cast again and got him, a nice ten-incher, bright with the glowing colors of the breeding male brookie–bright orange underside and snow white edging on the fins. I let him go. And then, as so often happens, I caught the next largest trout in the hole. And then the next, and the next, and finally pulled in a two-incher, flapping for all it was worth. It was time to move to where I could cast into another shadow.

Walking the rim, I made my way toward the east end of the dam, my eyes on the water. When I came to the little spillover rivulet, I stepped over it–and fell. A twig, or a series of them, bent under my foot and I flopped full length onto the outside of the dam. My feet disappeared into the mud and sticks. *slap!* went the beaver yet again.

I was still sliding down into the interior of the dam. The six-inch spillway sent a sharply cold stream of water across my neck and shoulder. I took hold of two of the larger branches in the dam and heaved. Nothing happened. My feet were caught. I struggled in sudden panic, but they would not move. The lattice of woven branches held them fast.

Belatedly, I realized that the water from the narrow spillway was running down into the waders. They were full of heavy, cold water to the knees. Quickly I moved my shoulders to the side and stopped the inflow. The waders were already heavy.

A light came on and I thought, "I will just slide out of these waders and then I will be out of this mess." I tried to shrug off the straps but could not manage it. The waders were caught firmly around the ankles by the invisible branches in the lower dam—and I had pulled the wader straps so tight to be able to wear them at all, that I could not get free. In sudden horror, I realized two things. One, the let-out sliders of the shoulder straps were behind my back, and two, I was sinking.

I struggled in panic and tried again to free my feet, but only succeeded in driving myself several inches further into the unseen mud of the bottom of the dam. I had dropped down an additional foot or more, and the water poured relentlessly onto my head. I tried to twist to the side but couldn't stay that way for long. And I continued to sink.

Gradually, the branch I had been holding with both hands, shifted and pulled from the dam. The cold water inside the waders was halfway up my thighs and I couldn't feel my feet any more. My eyes came level with the older part of the dam. I grasped a whitened branch and thought, "This is an old dam. There are countless feet of old, muddy silt under this dam." I tried to keep my elbows out so I wouldn't sink farther, but I could feel my arms shaking with the strain of holding myself up.

The hot August sun beat down on my arms, but inside I was cold. I began shivering. One elbow gave, and I slumped to the side. I was now shoulder deep in the dam and still sinking.

"Why, I am going to die here," I thought, surprised. "I will drown in the mud and die here." And I began to thrash and struggle with all my strength. More water poured into the waders. Now they were impossibly heavy. They dragged me down.

Above, the blue sky was a ragged hole rimmed with black branches and wavery with a skein of clear water pouring from it like a strange pale shawl. I breathed in and coughed and shivered. At once an upwelling of mud surged into the hole I had made in the dam, and it pressed the waders close to my body, a tight embrace. The water in them rose to the top. The mud forced its way upward to my waist. I scrabbled at the dam with my hands, but the branch I grabbed, though stout, broke free.

I looked at the round stick of wood I held, pointed on one end by the chisel marks of beaver teeth, smooth and speckled with pink and purple. Beaverwood, that kind of wood was called, and the colored speckles were formed somehow by the wood's being buried in water and mud while it was still green. People prized beaverwood and made lamp bases and picture frames from it. My piece was too small to make into a lamp. I almost let it go. The mud was up to my neck now, and it was difficult to breathe. In ten minutes, I would be cold and dead, just another buried log in a big beaver dam in Trail Creek bottom, *missing*. No one would ever find my body.

Almost without thinking I jammed the pointed end of the beaverwood under one of my wader straps and pried, at the same time ducking that shoulder as far down as I could manage. Water poured over my head and splashed into the mud under my chin. The pointed stick dug into my flesh; a patch of bright blood appeared on the shoulder of my blouse.

And the strap slipped off. A moment more, and I was free of the waders, clawing and kicking my way out of the hole. Gasping and slick with mud, I pulled myself up to the rim of the dam, dislodging branches everywhere as I crawled. I was too weak to stand.

Slap! went the beaver's tail when he saw me. I had made a small breach in the top of the dam and as I sat there, it widened. Quickly I slithered down and pulled the waders from their hole–no easy task, as they were full of mud and water. If one shoulder strap had not hooked itself over a forked branch, I would have lost them in the bottomless hole.

For a long time I lay in the widening breach in the top of the dam, letting the cool water wash me and the waders clean of the mud that covered us. I rinsed the blood from the fabric of my plaid cotton blouse. At least the cloth hadn't ripped.

Slap! Slap! The beavers were agitated, swimming circles in the pond closer and closer to me, desperate to repair their dam before it was too late to save the carefully provisioned larder that would see them through the long winter. There is little water coming down Trail Creek in August, and what they had collected had to be preserved.

Finally, I realized this and, collecting my fly rod and slinging the waders across my back, I moved off the dam very slowly and with great deliberation. When I looked back, the beaver family was already hard at work, plopping new mud into the spillway I had widened, and poking in new twigs. They would save their pond.

The hot sun felt good; my clothes were dripping and I was still shivering as I crossed the big sedge meadow and climbed the dirt and rock trail up to the sagebrush bench where I had parked the Express. I broke down my fly rod and stowed it behind the seat.

Looking at the waders, I thought for a moment of leaving them there. But they were not my waders, they were Gramps'. With a sigh, I tossed them into the back of the truck and drove to the golf shed at Sun Valley. I sat on the grass for a long time and waited for the golf carts to come in.

And at sunset, when I was dry and felt like myself again, the last of the golf carts came to the golf shed. I cleaned them and plugged each one into a charger. My day's work done, I drove home.

When I pulled into our driveway, Mother and Gramps were

sitting on our front steps in the twilight, having a cold drink. "Did you catch anything, Danny?" Gramps asked. His small brown eyes were keen; I wondered if he guessed that it hadn't been an ordinary day.

"No keepers," I said carefully. "It's pretty dumb to fly fish beaver ponds in the middle of the day."

"Oh, Danny, your new shoes!" Mom exclaimed suddenly. "Oh, no! Well, you will just have to wear those until we can afford to get you another pair. They are still new; it's just that you will never get those mud stains out and they won't look nice at school." Her eyes accused me.

"I'm sorry, Mom," I said. "I forgot."

"Again," was all she said, but it hurt.

Gramps' sharp eyes had noticed the damp patch on the wooden pickup bed under his waders. "Well, so you used my waders!" he said as I handed him the keys to the Express.

I nodded, rubbing at my throbbing shoulder. There would be a big bruise there tomorrow, but it would hide under a shirt or blouse quite easily.

"I've always thought you should wear waders," he went on. I sat heavily on the concrete step beside him. My legs felt like folding lawn chair legs, not like my own. "When I see you fishing, you always look so cold with your bare legs in the water," Gramps said. "How about if I get you some waders just like mine?"

"If it's all the same to you, Gramps, I will take my chances with bare legs," I told him.

Years later, decades later, I told Mom about the waders and the beaver dam and the new tennis shoes. We were sitting on her patio, each with a tall glass of iced tea.

"I thought at the time it might have been something like that," she said, moving her glass so the ice tinkled. "But you were so timid about driving that I felt I had to let you go out by yourself when you would go." She paused again. "I found blood on the plaid blouse you wore that day when I took it out of the laundry basket to put into the wash."

"But I rinsed it out!" I said, remembering.

"I found the blood on the inside," she said. "One shoulder seam was black with dried blood, underneath. You always told me nearly everything," she said with a faraway look in her eyes. "But you didn't tell me about that day. You didn't tell me because something dangerous happened," she told me. "You didn't want me to tell you that you couldn't drive out on your own."

"Yes," I said. "That was it."

"It was hard to let you go," she said.

Tony and the Other Face of the River

Wood River flowed through my Idaho home town like an ongoing conversation. I could always hear it. By running eight blocks downhill and trotting across a sagebrush meadow, I could be there, standing on cobblerock with my toes touching the water.

Our family fished in Wood River, often. We occasionally camped beside it miles above town. And sometimes we Ketchum girls and boys took inner tubes and floated there, in the less wild stretches. Or we had picnics on its rocky banks, or looked for tadpoles and frogs there, or built fairy houses of leaves and sticks on the river's gravel bars. Wood River was part of our lives, just like the dirt road down to Judy's house, or the agate place, or the Fourhills, or the frog pond. The river was familiar, a family friend. But during high-water snowmelt, Wood River was different.

When I was in the fourth grade, the river took one of my classmates, Arthur Black. Mom told me that Arthur had gone out to get a bucket of water from the river after school. In those days, of course, not everyone in Ketchum had indoor plumbing. Arthur had dipped the bucket, holding tightly to the handle, and the strength of the current had pulled him in. Arthur drowned. Neighbors searched the river in the dark with Coleman lanterns and flashlights. They found his body hours later, cold and white. I asked Mom, "But why didn't Arthur let go of the bucket? Why did he hang on? Why didn't he think to let go?"

"The river is fast, Danny," she said. "You might be surprised."

Only a few weeks before, Arthur had shyly brought me a birthday present, the book *Heidi*. The book was still there in my small bookcase when I learned that he had drowned, and it seemed very strange that the book was still there but Arthur was gone. At this distance of years I remember a tall, lanky boy with dark hair, fair skin, and earnest eyes. I remember that I told Arthur in front of the other children that it was wrong to say "loomnum" when he meant "aluminum." I wished I could tell him I was sorry for making fun of how he said "loomnum." It's been more than sixty years since Wood River took him, and still I remember. And am still sorry.

When I was fifteen, I almost had my chance to meet Arthur again and tell him. It was again high-water snowmelt. My horse, Tony, had been home from winter pasture for only a few days, and I was excited about taking a long Saturday ride, the first long ride of the year. I packed a lunch, saddled Tony, and took off over the hill.

Tony was too much horse for me. Everyone said so, and my parents were nervous about my taking off alone on Tony from the time I bought him until I gave him to a family friend ten years later. Tony came into my possession under a ruse. I was not supposed to have a horse like him.

I had saved my money for what seemed forever, and at last had a hundred and fifty dollars. Every spring a Ketchum man named Fred Miles went to horse sales in Nevada and in Twin Falls, and brought as many as twenty saddle horses to Ketchum to offer for sale to those families who didn't go to horse sales. Mr. Miles had just come from a sale. Money in hand, Dad and I drove down to his corrals, so close to Wood River that mosquitoes were out even in the daytime.

I saw Tony at once, and wanted him. My first two horses had been, truth to tell, old plugs. Here was a small, clean-limbed dapple gray, with smart black legs, mane and tail, and a love-ly, chiseled head. "That one," I said from my perch on the log fence of the corral.

"We-e-ell, little lady," said Mr. Miles, "that there gelding is three-fourths Quarter Horse, but he's one-fourth Arabian. That's why he's not very big, maybe only 800 pounds or so. He's a good size for the likes of you. And best of all, he has what they call the running walk. It's almost as fast as a trot, but smooth. Doesn't beat you to death like a trot does, and doesn't make him tired. When they find out about that, all the cowboys in town will be after this horse. However, he's only three years old. Might be a bit of a handful."

"Oh, Daddy, I want him!" Of course, I was hooked.

My father went to the gray gelding and ran a hand down his neck. "He is pretty," Dad said, "and I like it that he's small. Not so far to fall, Danny! But." Dad came to a full stop and thought a bit before he answered. "Here's the deal. We'll go home and get our stuff. Danny, if you can saddle and bridle him yourself, and ride him home through town, we'll take him." Dad looked at Fred Miles and looked hard. "That OK with you, Fred? When Danny gets him home, I'll come back and pay you."

"Sure, Stew. That's OK with me."

I could hardly breathe during the short ride home to get the tack, and I was still breathless with excitement when we got back to Mr. Miles' corral. Trying hard to look casual, I held out the bridle in what I hoped was a very cowboylike way and eased the bit into the gelding's mouth. He was quite relaxed and stood still with his head level so it was easy for me to reach over his ears. Saddling was easy, too. I swung into the saddle, waved to Dad and Mr. Miles, and rode off down the dirt lane, away from the river trees, and up into town.

Fifteen minutes later I was home, and I had a horse. I spent the rest of the day brushing him. I said every name I could think of to my new horse, since Mr. Miles hadn't known if he had a

Tony on a high ridge above Wood River north of
Ketchum. Tony was 3/4 Quarter Horse, 1/4 Arabian,
and a handful.

name. When I said Andy, Tommy, or Tony, he would prick up his ears. I named him Tony. I couldn't wait until my friends saw that I had a real horse now, one that even a cowboy would be proud to own.

The next morning, I took the saddle and bridle from the shed, and got quite a surprise. This time, Tony did not hold his head still for the bridle. He lifted his front legs and knocked me down flat. It took me two hours to get the bridle on him. By then, Tony's neck was hot and wet, and I was bruised and breathing hard. The saddle was another matter. Try as I might, tie him up every way I could think of, I could not saddle him. Eventually Dad and Gramps found me, purple-faced and stubborn, still trying to saddle my new horse.

Dad was not amused. He and Gramps eventually got the saddle onto Tony, but Dad's mouth was tight when he went into the house to phone Mr. Miles.

He came out ten minutes later, still grim-faced. "Well?" Gramps asked. "What did Miles have to say for himself?"

"It's what you thought. The horse was drugged yesterday. 'Gave him a little something to calm him down,' was the way he put it. I told him I ought to come down there and give him a Shoshone sandwich. He might think again with his teeth halfway down his throat. This horse is only green broke, if that. Danny could have been killed, riding him home through town. Stupid old bird—did he think we wouldn't notice? Danny, this is no horse for a young girl. This is a cowboy's horse. We'll take the saddle off and you can lead the horse down to Miles's corral and leave him there. I'll go later and get your money."

"Oh, but Dad!" I was devastated and very silly, as young girls often are where horses are concerned. He shouldn't have said that Tony was a cowboy's horse. "He's a good horse. He's just young. I know we can get him trained! Please! Please let me keep Tony!"

The three of us sat on the top bar of the log corral and had a long talk while Tony rolled his eyes at us, tied to the rail. Gramps agreed to get Tony tack-broken. I would help. I promised to ride him for two hours every day, even on school nights, to keep him "ridden down" so he wouldn't try anything funny with me. After a while, Dad drove down to Mr. Miles's corral and came back with a small smile and the better part of my money, which went straight into my college savings account. But I had, after all, bought myself a horse.

Tony learned fast, but he was very skittish for the first 20 years of his life. I should not have been allowed to keep him. It was like giving a fifteen-year-old the keys to a Ferrari. For years, when riding, once on him I stayed on him if at all possible, until I got home. I even ate my lunch on Tony's back. If I got off or was bucked off, it would be at least an hour's dance to get myself back onto him. At times Tony would see things he didn't like and either bolt or shy sideways at the speed of light. I learned much from Tony, mostly about how to read the moods of horses so I could stay on. He did have that fabulous running walk, and for years, cowboys would sit on the top rail of our corral, watch Tony walking, and make offers for him. I was very proud of Tony, though lucky to survive him.

This particular Saturday came in late May in the second year I had Tony.

Several unseasonably warm days in a row had sent meltwater from the snows of the Boulder Mountains racing down Wood River until it was high, muddy, and very, very fast. In summer, if you chose your place well, you could ride a horse across the Wood. But not today. Whole trees had been torn from the banks and were whirling along in the swift current. The river was loud with grinding, rolling rocks. I knew the water would be very cold.

Tony and I rode briskly around the hill, past the cemetery, northwest for half a mile on the dirt airstrip, across the highway, and down to Wood River. We would ride up Adams

Gulch today, I thought. I loved Adams Gulch with its small stream, groves of aspen and fir, and great pink cliffs. To get to Adams Gulch, we had to go across the Flowers bridge, so called because the Flowers brothers lived there and ran a little sawmill at the mouth of Adams, just across the river.

Tony and I had been over the bridge before, and I knew he didn't like it, even on the best of days. I could tell by the way he put down his feet and picked them up too quickly that he hated the hollow sound his steps made on the wooden planks. He would always walk carefully almost all the way across the bridge and then near the far side, would lunge the final twenty feet in a great leap or two, as if water demons were after him. I knew I had to be ready for that.

Tony walked warily onto the bridge. I could tell from his flattened ears that he didn't like the sound of the river today. I looked over the low parapet to see a great cottonwood snag, crowned with jagged branches, sliding under the bridge fast, surrounded by foam in water the color of hot chocolate.

Tony saw a small rock on the bridge near his front feet, a white piece of gravel no larger than half a golf ball, and he didn't like that either, so in a heartbeat, he shied to the side. This took us off Flowers bridge and into the air.

We hit the water with a *boom*. We went under and the cold shocked me. I had my eyes open under the water: there was no time to shut them, and everything was dark and brown.

Then we were on the surface, and Tony was swimming for the far bank. The great cottonwood snag revolved and hit Tony a glancing blow on one rear leg and turned him downriver. I held on and Tony stretched his neck flat and swam for all he was worth. At some point I realized that I still held the reins and directed him to a little cove.

With a tremendous heave, Tony hauled us out of the river. He blew down his nostrils and then, saddle, me, and all, he shook like an earthquake. I was too wet to care. We were both shivering; I could feel him shaking right through the saddle. I slid off, put both arms around his neck, and leaned the full length of my body down Tony's neck, chest, and front leg. He was warm.

We stood a long time beside the river, our feet inches deep in last year's dry cottonwood leaves. The river sound filled the world, and the air around us was chilled. This wasn't the friendly, clear river that we had camped beside so many times, where we had splashed in the shallows, where we had waded across at low water in the fall. I stared at the roiling waves of brown. This river was like a dragon. "I'm sorry, Arthur," I said.

On Tony's leg, a large welt rose beneath his hide, a welt as big as my hand, and when I led him a few feet, he limped. So I led Tony all the way home, both of us muddy, cold, and still shivering.

Mom saw me go through the corral gate and put Tony and his tack away, watched me rub him down with the blanket. "Better change those clothes before your father gets home," she said when I came up to the house, "and put them in the laundry basket down deep."

The Animals Isn't All Found Out

"The animals is all found out, Danny," Gramps told me when I was fourteen years old. He told his opinion as a story.

"A man said that to me when I was a little boy walking across Camas Prairie in the spring," Gramps said, leaning back into his easy chair, "and I believe it's true. You see, I was supposed to walk straight home from my uncle's house that day. I had stayed there for a few days playing with my cousin. I was about six years old, and it was less than ten miles between our two houses. I could have made it home easily before dinnertime. But I had my fishing pole with me that day, and I stopped to fish. I caught some, too, so I knew Mom wouldn't be too mad when I was late. Dad was gone on a trip to Boise with our team and wagon."

I settled myself on the carpet near Gramps' feet, ready to listen. I loved his stories.

"There had been a lot of snow that winter," he went on, "and the prairie was swampy, full of snowmelt ponds, some of them hundreds of acres, but not deep at all, with the tops of the grasses poking out. Huge rafts of ducks and geese were everywhere. Walking around some of those big pools slowed me down.

"And then there was one of those sunsets." He sighed. "One of those evenings when the whole sky was striped with orange clouds just like they were on fire, and the whole thing was reflected in a great big pond. I knew I should be moving on but

150

I stopped to rest and look at the sunset. It really was something else. But then I saw an animal coming through the water straight toward me. With the sunset behind it, the thing looked black, and I couldn't tell what it was."

The thing was coming toward him, straight toward him, arrowing through the water. Before long he could make out parts of it, or so he thought, and it was like nothing he had ever seen.

The thing in the water had three horns, but they weren't equal. One horn was long and thin, like a stick. The horn in the center looked like some sort of knob. Another horn was wider and shaped like a paddle. And the whole head was lumpy and uneven and huge. Gramps thought, "What is this animal?" It was like an elk, but it wasn't an elk. It was like a deer, but it wasn't a deer. It was most of all like a moose, yet it was different. Gramps moved back from the edge of the pool and crouched near the base of a small willow. He wanted to see this animal up close, but he didn't want it to see him. He didn't want to spook the thing and have it run away before it reached dry land. And what if it had sharp teeth and claws?

Now he could see the glint of ripples pushed in front of the creature as it continued toward him through the water, and he could hear the *slap, slap, slap* of new waves on the shore as the disturbance of the animal's passage ruffled the pool.

Yes, this was a big animal. But it was certainly not an elk or a moose. The head was all wrong, looking more wrong the closer it came. This animal was something new!

He waited in the deepening twilight. Though he was alone, he was not afraid. Great excitement filled him. He had heard of brave explorers finding new animals in the uncivilized places of the world. Camas Prairie wasn't very well explored, and certainly the surrounding mountains still had their secrets. With its bristling horns, this new animal would make 'em all stand up and shout, he thought.

151

By then he could hear the animal breathing great lungfuls of air, puffing as it swam steadily toward his beach. The black silhouette of the misshapen head looked even more strange as it came closer, and one of the horns seemed shiny. What would the body be like? A bear? A horse? Or could it even be like an elephant, or a camel?

The big animal came splashing through the shallows to shore. Small Gramps held his breath. The body was narrow and pale, very odd. He couldn't figure it out. And then its head fell off!

Gramps gasped in surprise. His splendid new animal was a man, and the man was stark naked.

"What?" said the man, equally startled. "Is somebody here?"

Gramps stood up to show himself. "It's just me," he said. "I thought you were an animal." In the clear twilight he looked down at the large "head" that he had seen swimming toward him. One horn was a saddle horn. The paddle-shaped horn was the curved top of a boot. The thin, sticklike horn was a rifle barrel.

The naked man sat in the grass and proceeded to unroll a bundle of clothes he had tied to his saddle. He began getting dressed. "What's your name, son?" he asked.

"Orly."

"Well, Orly, I lost my horse a good ways back and got tired of walking," said the man. "I went around some of this water, but this here lake seemed so big that I thought I would just walk right through it. But what do you mean, you thought I was an animal?"

"Your stuff on your head stuck out just like horns," Orly told him. "You looked like a moose, only different. I thought you were a whole new different kind of animal. I was very excited. I was going to be a discoverer."

The man dragged one hand down a bristly jaw, considering. "I think the animals is all found out, Orly," he said at last.

"Sorry." And with that, the man shouldered his rifle and sad-dle, and walked away east into the twilight. Orly never saw him again.

Gramps finished telling me the story, and his bright brown eyes peered sharply over his glasses. "Do you think the animals is all found out, Danny? I guess they must be, because I haven't heard of or found anything new here in all my years, and I've been around since 1891."

"But there could be, Gramps. There could be," I said. "What if you explored in Africa, or in the Amazon, or way down deep in the ocean? I'll bet there are new animals there, things that no one has seen yet."

"Maybe," he said, shaking his head slowly, "if you went look-ing in one of those kinds of places. But not around here," he pronounced. "That guy was right. Here, the animals is all found out."

****

After many years of outdoor work, the reading of countless scientific papers, and attendance at many scientific meetings, I knew that the animals were not all found out. Many of my friends and colleagues discovered plants and animals new to science, named them, and published the information, bring-ing the new species into the lists of known species of the world —insects, fungi, trees, flowers, fish, reptiles and amphibians, mammals, and even a few birds—although, to give Gramps his due, most of these new species were discovered in exotic places. For more than 30 years, I worked in the Idaho desert, for 20-plus years as the biologist for the Idaho Army Nation-al Guard. It was my job to help the Guard keep the military training area in good shape, to protect the rare species there, to restore damaged areas with native plants, to help the various colonels design soldier training exercises so that minimal damage to the environment would result, and to monitor the health of the ecosystem to make sure that the plants and animals were holding their own.

I needed to know what species occurred on the training area, and every time I found something I couldn't identify, I would send specimens to someone who was an expert in that group, to make sure that the plant or creature was identified accurately. To manage an ecosystem, you have to know what is being managed.

Every year I'd hire a field crew of college students. I and my senior technician, Jay, would be out in the desert with them all summer (and much of the fall) in 4x4 vehicles, monitoring the more than 250 permanent vegetation transects so we could determine which areas and plants were thriving, which areas needed rest, and which areas could use some restoration. We did all kinds of field science—discovering the effects of different intensities of tank travel on shrublands, determining which kinds of small animals lived in which kinds of vegetation, and most importantly, we documented the life history of a rare white wildflower called slick-spot peppergrass, *Lepidium papilliferum*, which is not a grass, but looks like a bunchy variety of sweet alyssum, except that it truly is peppery and not at all sweet.

Every year in April, we would collect flowers, rocks, and branches from the training area, plus a few small creatures like lizards and deer mice, and set up a display for the soldiers at the home base on Gowen Field in Boise as part of a celebration of Earth Day. Easy additions to the annual celebration were fairy shrimp. They were interesting and could be poured into an aquarium for an almost instant display.

Fairy shrimp in Idaho are seasonal creatures, and in the desert, they occur when there is water in the temporary pools, or playas. This happens in late fall, winter, and early spring. Raking the water with their feathery leg-scoops, they feed upon algae and tiny aquatic creatures like ostracods and copepods, even under thick ice in the dead of winter. By late spring in most years, the water has evaporated and the playas are dry as dust, and remain that way, the playa-bed soils cracking as they bake in the summer heat, until the rains come in late autumn. In many years, the playas do not fill at all, and there are no shrimp.

Luckily for the shrimp, however, their eggs can withstand years—even decades—of desiccation, and are brought to life by the cold fall rains.

One year, the playas filled with water in the late fall and held water until mid-April. Jay and I drove out into the training area to collect some shrimp for the annual Earth Day event. But most of the playas we visited—Tadpole Lake, Range 22 Lake, Davis Peppergrass Lake, Flamingo Lake, and others—had no shrimp that spring.

Then we remembered a large playa near the southeastern boundary of the Guard training area, one we called Armadillo Lake because of its odd shape. We hadn't netted for shrimp in Armadillo before, but on that day, we were in luck. Armadillo Lake, though its water was brown and opaque, had shrimp.

We were used to seeing several species of small fairy shrimp, half-inchers or smaller, most of them pale cream-colored creatures, curling along with beating legs under their curved backs—little guys. But in Armadillo that day, we found something else.

This shrimp was large—huge for a fairy shrimp, almost three inches long. Instead of small, fat tail segments, this one was unlike any of the others, with a straight, divided tail looking rather like a two-tined barbeque fork, and it had *claws*.

It was obvious to us as we dumped the first one into the collecting jar, that this thing was different, and that we had netted a predator. We collected several shrimp of both kinds and took them back to our lab on Gowen Field Base, where we fished them from the jar of brown water and put them into a dishpan of clear water.

Immediately, the large shrimp began to hunt, capture, and eat the smaller shrimp species. It was that simple. I had seen these large fellows a few times many years in the past as I worked in the desert but had never collected any. In Idaho, the animals had all been found out, hadn't they?

After some searching, we found an online key to the species of fairy shrimp in the West. A giant species did exist, and it occurred in Oregon, *Branchinecta gigas*. But the Oregon species had a short, blunt tail and didn't look anything like our large fellows. The smaller one we identified easily; it was a common species, found all over the West. But the large one would not key out.

Jay and I weren't crustacean experts, and at first we thought the problem was with us, that we didn't know fairy shrimp anatomy well enough to work the key successfully. But after several weeks, both of us came to the conclusion that our three-inch guy was not in the key. We needed an expert.

The expert we found was Christopher Rogers, a biologist living a thousand miles away. Our first conversation on the phone was unsatisfying. "Oh, if it's that big, it's the Oregon species, *gigas*," he said.

"But the tail!" I protested. I wasn't as calm as I should have been.

After several minutes during which we were both becoming more and more frustrated, Christopher said, "Hey, why don't you pickle a few and send them to me. I'll have a look at them and call you back."

That sounded good. Our captured shrimp were dying any-way, not doing well in the clear water. Several of the large shrimp went into vials of alcohol and, carefully labeled, were mailed to Christopher. Jay and I waited impatiently.

One morning as I unlocked my office, I heard the phone ring-ing and got myself inside just in time to answer it. It was Christopher, and he was shouting.

"Dana!" his voice boomed from the receiver. "Dana! Dana!"

Christopher had received our package. He knew the western species of fairy shrimp well, all the species of fairy shrimp. And ours wasn't one of them. We had found a species new to science!

In our government Jeep Cherokee, we slithered over the muddy dirt road to Armadillo Lake and captured a few more specimens.

My husband, Scott, set up lights on a tank and videotaped our shrimp as they pursued, captured, and ate the smaller species. Scott sent the video to Christopher on CD. Christopher was indeed an expert; he himself had described several new species of fairy shrimp over the years, but never a savage little monster like this!

Christopher, Jay, Scott, and I, plus a fellow biologist from Denmark with access to an electron microscope, Jorgen Olesen—worked on the description of the anatomy, habitat, and behavior of our new species. We found that the eggs of the females were bright turquoise blue. Scott was the first to discover that when prey became scarce, our species would stockpile food by attaching the living prey shrimp to its abdomen with Velcro-like spines, eating them one by one. And Jorgen's work with the electron microscope revealed that our creature sported many kinds and countless rows of strange spines not visible to the naked eye.

Christopher, Jorgen, Jay, and I wrote our findings into a paper, which was published in the *Journal of Crustacean Biology*. Our new species was now official. Since the only known locations were inside the Snake River Birds of Prey National Conservation Area, and since the creature is such a formidable predator, we named it *raptor, Branchinecta raptor*. The paper was published in 2006, and is still one of the most-cited papers on fairy shrimp.

As I was listening to Christopher shouting my name through the phone receiver, I couldn't help thinking of Gramps. Twenty years before, at the age of 96, Gramps had left us. "The animals isn't all found out," I thought as I listened to Christopher telling me our species was new to science. I wished I could show Gramps our strange and spiky creature, found only 30 miles from the largest city in Idaho, a new species in our own back yard. Who knows what else is out there?

Shag, His Saga

Shag was Dad's horse for a while. A big, strong dark brown with a narrow blaze, Shag was born on Castle's ranch near Carey, a lovely place snuggled up to the foothills of the Muldoon Mountains.

Bill Castle had a two-mile-square pasture for some of his horses. Shag was born there and was gelded young. The summer he was a yearling, Shag ran with his dam, several other mares and colts, and the herd stallion, in this large, wild pasture.

One day Bill saw two men stop their truck along the fence, aim their rifles, and shoot into the pasture. Bill rushed toward them, but by the time he got there, they had sped away in an old pickup. He looked at the horses. "The big brown colt was down," he told us. "I went and got my sons and we ran out to the colt. He saw us and spooked. We could see blood running down his neck and dripping off his chest, but he wouldn't stop trying to get away from us. We couldn't get close enough to rope him. Finally, we decided that we'd kill the colt if we kept chasing him, so we just left him. And he made it, but he wouldn't let us touch him from then on. We could see through binoculars that he had one hell of a scar on his neck. He was a tough one, that colt. We called him Savage after that."

About four years later, Dad and Bill were talking one day when we were visiting the ranch, and Dad said, "I like the look of your Quarter Horses, Bill, but I'm looking for a bigger fellow so I can pack out an elk on him. Do you have anything?"

Bill scraped a hand down the length of his jaw. Finally, he squinted toward the wild pasture and said, "Well, there's Savage. He's the big guy on that little ridge there in the sage. He's as wild as they come. If you can take him, Stew, you can have him." The men shook on it.

I was sixteen, and watched in awe as the big, heavily muscled horse came galloping down the ridge to join the other horses in a draw. His black mane fell to his knees, and his tail dragged the ground until it was lifted by the wind of his speed. To me, it seemed so romantic—taming a wild horse.

The grunting, sweating reality was a bit different. The following weekend, Bill's sons saddled up and drove the pasture horses into a corral. Savage was roped and a leather halter wrestled onto his head. He stood blowing down his nostrils, his legs rigid and trembling. I could see the wide, twisted scar on one side of his neck, sunk into a fleshy hollow big enough to take a man's fist: the place where the bullet had exited, blowing out a blob of muscle just under his spine.

It took eight men and four ropes, five hours, and broken horse trailer doors, to get Savage into our trailer. Gramps, expert with untamed horses, had come to the ranch with Dad and me to get Savage, and Bill and his sons had called in some neighbors as well.

The struggle was epic, and Savage was dripping white lather by the time the men had hauled him partway into the trailer. The sound of his front feet clopping on the wooden floor of the trailer panicked him, and he charged into the trailer, hit the front wall with his forehead, and fell unconscious, backward. The men shrugged, had a close look at Savage, brought a pickup with a winch—and soon Savage had been dragged into the trailer. Many turns of thick rope secured the broken doors. As I said, it was epic.

Dad muttered on the way home. "I must be nuts. What are we going to do when he wakes up? And how the hell are we going to get him shod? He's never had shoes. We've broken colts just fine, but how are we going to break this huge five-year-old without getting ourselves killed?" After a few miles of silence, he announced, "And we're not going to call him Savage. No. He's got so much hair—I'm going to call him Shag."

We deposited Shag at our friend George Castle's ranch (George, brother of Bill) up Lake Creek, in a sturdy log corral, a stronger corral than we had at home. Shag burst out of the back of the trailer, sending the doors flying, and stood in the center of the corral, showing the whites of his eyes. He was terrified of the logs, the water barrel, the manger—everything. However, he was fine with George Castle's gentle mare, Nellie. We had put Nellie into the corral to help Shag feel at home, and it did help.

Shag quickly became used to the routine up Lake Creek. Nearly every day that summer I rode my horse, Tony, the five miles from our house to Lake Creek. I taught Shag to have his mouth handled, and his ears, and to be brushed. It took me a couple of weeks to detangle that magnificent mane and tail, and when I lifted the mane, I found an enormous, foot-long scar, and for the first time realized just how close a call that bullet had been. On the bare side of Shag's neck, the scar with the big hollow in the neck muscle was four inches below his spine, but on the side covered by his mane, the scar was barely an inch away from the vertebrae.

I began picking up his giant, cracked hooves and tapping on them to get him ready for the farrier. It turned out that Shag was really very gentle and steady. Gramps decided to do the shoeing himself, though he hadn't shod a horse for forty years, and that went well, too. I began throwing a blanket over Shag. Then came the saddle. And finally, the saddle with the cinch. No worries.

At last came the day of the first ride. I got the saddle and bridle on Shag. He swiveled his ears, knowing something was up, because our whole family was sitting on the corral logs with bated breath. Dad pretended not to be apprehensive as he put a boot into the stirrup.

In a flash, Dad was aboard. And Shag, formerly Savage? He just stood there. He did nothing. After a minute or two, he ambled slowly around the corral. We couldn't believe it. He didn't even blink when we all cheered.

Shag was a calm and steady saddle horse, but never learned to neck rein very well. If you wanted him to turn, you had to pull the rein on that side. Shag was big and strong, but he had a serious drawback as a pleasure horse. He would not budge from the corral unless another horse was with him. It would have taken a tank to drag him out the gate. And if another person rode with Dad, Shag would not walk side by side with the other horse unless Dad turned himself into a windmill of kicking legs and flailing arms—not the most dignified way to ride! Shag would walk contentedly with his nose to the other horse's tail. Mostly. But sometimes, Shag went into a sudden state where he WOULD NOT GO. Not for nothin'—not no-how. You'd have to get off and lead him for a couple of miles. If you tried to get on too soon, he WOULD NOT GO. He was not the ideal saddle horse.

One day a couple of years or so later, our friend Sandy Brooks came for a visit, and as he and Dad had drinks while sitting on the porch in the late-summer twilight, Sandy said, "That's a nice-looking big guy there in the corral, Stew."

And Dad said, "Shag is as strong as an ox, but he will walk only behind another horse."

Sandy took a pull of his bourbon and said, "Stew, that guy belongs in a pack string. A trail string. Be nice to have a gelding that big to carry my woodstove when I'm packing into the lakes in the White Clouds with clients." Sandy had a ranch in the

Stanley Basin, and in the summer supplemented his income by taking clients on delightful pack trips into the Sawtooth and the White Cloud Mountains. Many of his clients went for the fly fishing as well as the scenery, and Sandy liked to serve them gourmet meals, including their own fresh fish, cooked on a folding metal stove.

"Got something to trade?" Dad asked.

This is how we got beautiful Bonnie, a flashy little sorrel filly fresh from Sandy's ranch.

The following week, Sandy showed up on a Saturday morning with his trailer. After talking to Gramps about how to get Shag into a trailer, Sandy left Bonnie in his trailer while loading Shag. That loading was boring rather than epic. Then Bonnie came out into our corral, and Shag went over the mountains to Sandy's ranch.

We were told that Shag looked bored when the big stove was loaded onto his pack, and he did well as a pack horse for the rest of that summer. "He can carry anything you can put on him," Sandy boasted on one occasion. "He truly is as strong as an ox."

Shag started out the next summer in the pack string and everything was fine—for a while.

One day Sandy, his clients, and his pack horses were headed up into the White Clouds for two weeks of fishing. They were climbing a steep trail through pale, broken talus, with a 500-foot drop on one side. Shag had done this before. Sandy wasn't worried. But he had yet to experience one of Shag's WILL NOT GO moments.

Shag was almost to the top of the talus slope when he had a WILL NOT GO moment. It was time for that stove to get off and walk for a while! But, of course, the stove did not understand.

Shag began to buck. He bucked and bucked while standing in place on the trail, hardly even pulling on the horse in front or the horse behind. Sandy began running down along the pack string to get to Shag.

But then, with a mighty effort, Shag bucked off the stove, and Sandy arrived at Shag just in time to see the stove, banging and clanging off the rocks, tumbling all the way to the bottom of the slope, now a useless, crumpled ball of metal. Shag shook himself a little and rubbed his head on Sandy's sleeve.

Sandy told us, "I said to myself, I don't care if he likes me, this is it! Two weeks with clients and without a stove! And when the whole string got to the top of the ridge where we could get off the trail, I stripped off the halter and the pack saddle, and popped him on the rear. And Shag turned around and took off back down the mountain."

We were a little shocked, but . . .

We looked for Shag the next time we went fishing in the Stanley Basin, and we saw him grazing along the Salmon River with a herd of cattle. We tried to get close, but he lifted that long tail and ran, flat-out, up to a bench and then galloped a mile on the sage flat there.

For at least ten years, Shag was a fixture in the Basin near Fourth of July Creek, sometimes ranging as far upstream as Beaver Creek and even Pole Creek. When anyone came close, he ran, mane and tail tangled once more and flying. In the springtime, he would look thin and ratty, but by autumn, he was always sleek and fat. How he made it through those deep-snow, forty-below winters at 7,000 feet, I cannot imagine.

Shag lived out his life in the basin. One time we'd see him in a herd of antelope. Another time, he'd be standing in the shade of a big pine with some rancher's horses, or we'd see him crossing the river all alone, flicking the end of his wet tail against the deer flies.

Then one year, we saw Shag no more. He lived as an outlaw until he was at least seventeen. In my mind's eye, all these years gone, I see him there still, galloping along the sage rim, a dark cloud with a halo of pale dust.

Gramps is gone, Dad is gone, Bill and George Castle are gone, Sandy Brooks is gone, and Shag is gone—along with Nellie, Bonnie, and Tony. But somehow I am still here, and I remember.

A Farewell

Growing up in Ketchum, Idaho when I did, everyone in town saw Ernest Hemingway almost every day. It was unavoidable. When he was in Idaho, every day that he wasn't fishing or hunting, Hemingway would trek into Ketchum from his house on Wood River just upstream from the mouth of Warm Springs Canyon: once to the post office and to buy a newspaper, and again later in the day, to the liquor store, carrying home a little something in a brown paper bag.

Everyone in town called him "Papa," except for Dad. Dad called him "Ernest."

When Sun Valley resort opened its doors in 1936, Mom and Dad were on board as two of the youngest full-time employees. Mom was a secretary. Dad was a fishing and hunting guide, seventeen years old. The other four original Sun Valley guides were men in their forties. One of Dad's first clients was Ernest Hemingway, and fly fishing was what they did together, for a number of years.

I have seen many fly fishermen and was a guide myself for several years, but I have never seen anyone as skilled as my father. He could read the water, read the fish, and cast farther, cast straighter, cast lighter, and cast more accurately than anyone I have ever seen. Add to this an encyclopedic knowledge of the local creeks, lakes, and canyons, unfailing patience, interest in everything outdoors, and a large scoop of kindness, and you

Dad fishing Silver Creek, where he often
guided Hemingway.

have a great fly fishing guide.

In those early days, Hemingway lived in the Sun Valley Lodge. Dad would drive to pick him up in one of Sun Valley's woody station wagons, and most often, they would fish the great shining loops of Silver Creek, hoping to hook a lunker rainbow lurking in the shadows under a swampy bank or a stubby willow.

Mom found herself pressed into service after Hemingway married the celebrated war correspondent Martha Gellhorn. Mom could rattle out over a hundred words per minute on one of those old manual typewriters and was hired to type the manuscript of one of Martha's books. Mom soon found herself typing part of *For Whom the Bell Tolls* for Papa himself.

Dad said that one early-autumn day, he and Hemingway drove down to Camas Prairie to do some target shooting, to sight in their rifles for hunting season. On the way home, they had a serious disagreement about a black cow.

After this, relations between Dad and Hemingway were cool. Dad never guided Hemingway again.

And then came the Great War. Dad and Mom married, and Dad ended up in the Navy, stationed on Catalina Island, off the coast of southern California, from which he made long voyages into the Pacific Theatre of World War II. I was born on the Navy base there.

After the war, my parents hurried home, and with the help of my mother's parents, built a small house on a gentle slope in Ketchum. Hemingway married again, to Mary Welsh, also a journalist.

As the years wore on, Dad and Hemingway became friendly once more, a kind of distanced respect, I think, plus the fact that in a town as small as Ketchum, rubbing shoulders had to happen. Hemingway would call Dad now and then for advice of a fishing and hunting nature, or to ask him if this or that person was someone who could be trusted. And occasionally, on freezing or rainy days when we were out and about in our Jeep, we'd see Hemingway on one of his daily walks and would pick him up and ferry him to his destination.

I never saw much of Hemingway, other than those occasional conversations in our Jeep. In the late '50s, Mary, who had spent most of her time with her new husband at their home in Cuba, came to live with him in the house on Wood River. She soon gathered a wide circle of local friends.

But things were not going well, somehow. We all knew that Hemingway was suffering increasing bouts of depression. However, he kept to his routines.

****

I remember the last time I encountered him. I was sixteen. On a below-zero winter day, Mom and I had just been to the West One Bank and were walking back to our car between snowbanks.

Hemingway saw us and crossed the street to intercept us. He took both Mom's hands in his and said, "Bernice, they're after me. I don't know how long I can hold out."

"Who is after you?" Mom asked.

He jerked his head in the direction from which he had come. "The FBI," he said. "See those men?" Across the street, leaning against a storefront, stood two men.

"Those men are with the FBI," Hemingway said.

Mom said, "Gosh, really?"

"I know it must seem far-fetched," Hemingway said, still gripping her wrists, "but they are tracking me." He let her go and said, "Wish me luck." He strode away.

"Good luck," Mom called after him, but he didn't look back. We hurried to the car. Mom started the engine, then looked toward the place where the men had been standing. They had gone.

"Do you think those guys are really FBI?" I asked.

Mom adjusted the heater vent. After a moment, she said. "They had on fedoras, city hats like your Gramps used to wear. They are wearing long wool overcoats. And I could see one man's shoes. He is wearing dress shoes, slick-bottomed dress shoes."

"Guys here wear parkas or big coats on days like this," I said slowly. "They wear different hats from those. Warm hats. And in the winter, nobody wears slick shoes."

Mom smiled and began to back out of the parking space. "It does seem far-fetched though. I mean, Papa is a writer. Why would the FBI be after a writer?"

A few months later, Hemingway was dead, having rigged his own shotgun and pulled the trigger.

Our town became crazy during the few days before the funeral. Reporters and newscasters of all sorts flooded Ketchum. News that Hemingway's death had been suicide was leaking out, and they were hungry for details. Hemingway's friends were hounded and traffic on our one-stoplight main street snarled and bunched. Mary Hemingway could not be found, though the reporters asked and asked, but we all knew where she was.

A day or two later, a small white envelope came in the mail: an invitation to the funeral. Mary had sent out fifty invitations, and the cemetery entrance would be guarded; only those with invitations would be allowed to attend.

Mary had been sequestered by her friends Chuck and Floss Atkinson in an apartment above their Atkinson's Supermarket, two blocks from our house. Eventually, reporters ferreted out Mary's whereabouts, and the telephone switchboard that serviced Atkinson's Grocery and their adjacent Christiana Motel, went wild. Mom walked down the hill and installed herself at the switchboard to help process the thousands of calls.

The day of the funeral dawned bright and hot, hotter than

the usual summer day, even for the 7th of July. "Too hot to live," Grandma Lily remarked as I ran down the grassy bank to saddle Tony. I felt stifled, and not just by the heat. The number of people in town was unprecedented, oppressive. I had to get out of town.

Tony and I took off up our dirt street, turned west at Clara Spiegel's house, and continued on around the south side of the Fourhills. We'd ride along the outside, the uphill side of the cemetery fence, and cross the flats a half mile to Eve's Gulch, I thought. Then we'd walk straight up the rocky gully where no car could go. At the top of the hills, we'd be alone, above all the strangeness. I knew a place where we could laze in the shade of a rock outcrop there. We could watch the traffic below at a distance, eat our lunch (I always packed food and drink for Tony as well as for myself), and I could read one of the books in the saddlebags.

I had thought the funeral was to be later that afternoon, but when Tony and I rounded the hill, the graveside ceremony had already begun. Tony's head came up, and I gathered the reins tightly. He was not the most reliable horse—far from it.

As we passed through a narrow neck of sagebrush and found the ill-defined path along the outside of the cemetery fence, the whole world seemed changed and alien. Someone had mowed the entire cemetery, and the wayward grasses and tall weeds had been shaved almost to the ground. Cars, parked nose to tail on the downhill side of the cemetery, lined the highway.

Along the east fence, a solid line of reporters stood shoulder to shoulder in the sage, leaning into the old wire fence, the heavy cameras on their shoulders grinding away in the midday heat.

Tony tossed his head and pinned back his ears. Somewhere behind us, a popcorn vendor had moved in and was setting up a cart. He put a bullhorn to his lips and shouted, "Popcorn! Ice cream! Popcorn!" Tony made a fractious little jump, and I

kneed him in the ribs. "Calm down, Tony," I said. "Let's walk."
Tony stepped out into his running walk.

Halfway along the length of the cemetery fence, I stopped
Tony to see if I could find Dad. Mom wouldn't be there; she was
still at the switchboard. I saw Mary in her fashionable black
dress and wide black hat, escorted by a man I didn't know. The
ceremony was Catholic, and I recognized Father Waldman and
several altar boys, little fellows clad in puffy white blouses and
billowy skirts.

Hemingway was to be buried near the center of the cemetery.
I had arrived just as the pallbearers laid the coffin down near
the dark rectangular hole, half-hidden by flowers. I found Dad
at last, in the back row of mourners near an arrangement of
spiky gladiolas. I felt sorry for him, bundled into his dark suit
on such a hot afternoon.

Then, commotion. One of the altar boys, Cliffy Goicochea,
suddenly collapsed onto the grass, unconscious. People broke
ranks and ran to him.

This was too much for Tony, who bolted along the fence path,
and, at the far end of the cemetery, broke into a wild gallop. I
leaned forward and let him go; I had had enough, too.

Tony and I spent the rest of the day on the rounded ridgetop
between Sun Valley and the next gulch north from Eve's Gulch,
the one I called Echo Valley, sheltering from the baking sun
under a leaning outcrop of rhyolite. We each ate a sandwich
and drank a bottle of Pepsi.

In the late afternoon when I could see the traffic thinning,
when most of the cars had left the cemetery area, Tony and I
walked down onto the flats and made our way home.

Very quickly, life in Ketchum went back to what passed for
normal. Hemingway's stone arrived, a huge, flat slab of dark
granite, simply engraved. Before long, Mary Hemingway
decided that she needed to learn to drive, so Dad taught her,
on those same dusty flats where Tony had galloped away from

the funeral.

For years after, when Tony and I were coming home in the chilly darkness after a long day's ride in the hills, I'd ride into the cemetery, let Tony graze nearby, and I would sit on Hemingway's stone to get warm before heading home around the flank of the Fourhills. Something dark like that will hold the heat.

Blood Moon and the Band of Gold

I was a sophomore at Hailey High School, I was sixteen, and I was in the Pep Club. It was the Pep Club's mission to support our football and basketball teams.

To each game, Pep Club girls wore raglan-sleeved white sweaters with a large green "H" sewn to the fronts, white and green knife-pleated vertically-striped short skirts, and white tennis shoes with green ankle socks. The sweaters were identical except for size, but the skirts were not as uniform, because each of us had received a length of striped cotton fabric and from this had each made our own skirt, so each was a bit different, just like us girls. My friends, Barbara and Jackie, were in Pep Club, too, as were the majority of the other-than-freshman girls in Hailey High.

Part of Hailey High's Pep Club was a group of girls who performed as a drill team. Unlike drill teams and Pep Clubs today, then everyone willing and ambulatory could join, not just the lovely and coordinated, so we girls ran the gamut from large to small, tiny to tall, graceful to awkward, beautiful to ordinary. Our student instructor, Claudia, choreographed our drills and tried to whip us into some kind of precision. I am sure we were a great trial to Claudia. At least she had us all on the same foot most of the time! We didn't often perform at football games; basketball game half times were where we shone, since our drills were better seen in bright light and from

174

above. But as well as drill teaming, the whole Pep Club worked with the cheerleaders to perform intricate yells and responses during all Hailey's games. We considered ourselves necessary.

Occasionally, the school district would provide a school bus (in addition to the players' bus) for travel to an away game—a wonderful thing, since so few of us had cars. Our playing league was called The Little Six, and every away game we had was a *far*away game. The farthest was Glenns Ferry (120 miles) and the closest was Shoshone (50 miles). Since we passed through Shoshone every time we went to an away game, often on the way home the buses would stop there at the Manhattan Cafe, a homey little place where my parents and their friends had stopped after their own high school football and basketball games, for Cokes, fries, and burgers, just as we did ourselves. After many of the games, both the team bus and the Pep Club bus would stop at the Manhattan for almost an hour before returning to Hailey. I can still remember the tall, cocky guys in their green letterman's jackets, leaning over booths pink with giggling girls, everyone laughing and stuffing themselves with french fries dipped in ketchup.

One Friday night, an eager group of Pep Club girls rode the bus to a football game. We were not to march. Instead, we all sat in a block on the wooden bleachers and cheered for our team. This game was in Kimberly, a small farming town east of Twin Falls. That year the Hailey vs Kimberly game was one of the middle games of the season. It was late September, and the air that evening hung unusually heavy and still over the football game and over the nearby fields of wheat and corn stubble, and of newly dug potatoes. I can't remember if Hailey won or lost the game but was disappointed to hear that on this night we would not be stopping at the Manhattan on the way home. The game had had many timeouts, and it would be very late when we got home, even without a stop at the Manhattan.

Many of us Pep Club girls were in Chorus, the school's singing group. In those days, some activities were separated by sex, so Chorus was all female—disappointing, no doubt, to boys who had good singing voices. Often during the long after-game bus trips home in the dark, some of us would put our heads together and sing. We would start with songs we were practicing in Chorus, but then would bring out some old standbys everyone knew, like *Swing Low, Sweet Chariot* and *Beautiful Dreamer*. Later, we would pick up popular songs, like *My Special Angel, Blueberry Hill, Misty, Love Me Tender, Venus, Chantilly Lace, Sugartime,* and *Kisses Sweeter than Wine*.

On these late-night trips home through the tunnel of darkness, we seldom chose rollicking, lighthearted fare. We were young girls; we had just spent two hours watching our boys play hard, and perhaps for these reasons, nearly all the songs we sang on the bus home were songs of romance.

We were accustomed to singing together, and some of the girls sang lovely impromptu harmony. Those of us who wanted to sing would change places with those who wanted to talk or sleep, and we singers would cluster in the middle of the bus, often sitting on the edges of the seats and putting our heads together down the center aisle. Our sweet voices seemed to fill the bus with dreams.

Many of these girls were among the high school elite, those who would barely speak to girls like me in the halls of our school. Pretty girls with steady boyfriends had high status. Those ordinary girls like me, with no boyfriend, did not. But in the dark the popular girls seemed glad to have my good soprano, and I was glad of the anonymity of the darkness that brought the brief feeling of belonging. Hands laced over the high seats in front of us, chins on hands, all of us were equally pretty, equally popular in the dark.

Eventually all the girls would fall silent, alone with their thoughts or nodding off to sleep. But before that, we had to sing the last song. We bus girls had made a tradition of our own, unspoken and unbroken. There was one song that, as sleepy voices began to drop away, was always the last song to be sung. This song was *Band of Gold*.

There were three girls with wonderful voices, who knew all the words (plus verses they made up) and always sang *Band of Gold* to the end. Carol's voice was soprano, clear and true as a shining spear. Kris sang second-soprano, and her voice, while on perfect pitch, had a hint of softness at the edges that made it seem like watercolors. Nancy sang alto, a smoky, rich underpinning to the others. Many, many times I leaned my cheek against the cool smoothness of the bent pipe edging on the seat in front of me and floated away into fantasy, sleep, or both, to the chorus of *Band of Gold*, "Just a little band of gold, to tell me that you're mine."

That 1955 hit was old even then, but songwriter Kit Carson's words had found a place with us, and we sang *Band of Gold* every time we found ourselves on a school bus for a long time in the dark, when we were ready for silence or sleep. The older girls could sing every word of *Band of Gold* by heart, including their made-up verses, and so that made it very desirable for us younger girls to learn it, too. Knowing our version of *Band of Gold* was a kind of badge of belonging. *Band of Gold* was a song for midnight dreamtime, when the others could not see your face.

On the way home from Kimberly that night, my seatmate Barbara had fallen asleep early in the journey home. Barbara was also a member of Chorus and enjoyed singing on the bus, but on this night she had lasted only a few songs before she fell asleep. I was in the window seat and Barbara was near the aisle. She was a tiny little thing, and I was able to lean over Barbara and sing without disturbing her.

Outside, I knew, the waning moon was soon to rise, but for now the sky was blank and black, stars hidden by a high roof of cloud. Suddenly really hearing the words of one of the romantic songs, I thought of the future, the real future, perhaps considering this for the first time as a teenager. *Band of Gold* was indeed the dream of most of these girls, and since they had few career plans, it was *the* dream. I realized that for them it would be the band of gold or no dream at all—and after graduation, if not married soon, they would become shopgirls, secretaries, waitresses, or maids at Sun Valley resort and local motels. I don't think I had ever realized this before that night. Like so many girls, I dreamed of love and marriage (which in 1960 meant virtually the same thing to a teenage girl), but figured that these would not be mine, and I should plan for a solitary life. The band of gold, for me, was a dearly held dream, but I knew even then that it was only a dream. Nevertheless, with hidden face I, too, could dream that dream in the dark as the bus rolled along the familiar road north of Shoshone.

All was quiet on the bus. I could feel the highway through the hard-bottomed seat and resettled myself. The two girls on the seat in front, the ones across from me, and the girls just behind were breathing softly and regularly, asleep. The radium dial on my watch showed that it was straight-up midnight when Carol began *Band of Gold*. Nancy and Kris chimed in, and the soft melody drifted over my head toward the back of the bus. A few others joined us, mostly for the chorus: "a little band of gold, to tell me that you're mine." These weren't quite the correct words as written, but we always sang the chorus this way in the depth of a long night's journey home.

Resting my forehead on the window glass, I looked out the window. Something was happening outside, to the east. The cloud ceiling was lifting and breaking up. A few stars shone through. "Where's the moon?" I thought, for I was a creature of the night—even at sixteen—and knew that the waning moon must be soon to rise.

From the rolling plain of dark sage lifted a tiny eye of scarlet, becoming larger and larger until I realized with a shock that the misshapen, swollen light was the moon. The moon rose red as blood. I stared at the thing, my lips still moving to *Band of Gold.*

Why was the moon red? Could the world be ending? This seemed a real possibility in that era of Cold War nuclear threats and family bomb shelters. Or was the red moon an omen of evil to come? Should I wake the sleeping girls, tell the singers to look out the east windows, shout to our bus driver to hurry home? No, I said to myself, suddenly realizing what was happening. For one thing, there is always evil to come; no omen is necessary. I understood that even as a high school girl.

I realized then that the red moon was not a supernatural event, simply a message to the world that there was a fire to the east, with dense smoke near the ground. I remembered a forest fire that one afternoon had turned the sun red. I knew that many farmers burned crop stubble in the autumn, so no doubt somewhere to the east, this burning in the heavy air had dyed the moon the color of fresh blood.

And yet, as I looked out over the dark sagebrush desert and the sparse, winking lights of lonely farmhouses, I saw something. "There's something secret out there in that sagebrush, I'll bet," I was thinking. "Somewhere in this lava desert north of Dietrich, northeast of Shoshone, south of Craters of the Moon, where no one goes anymore, there's a ghost town no one has set foot in since the people went away. Or there's an unknown animal or flower that no one has ever seen." I could not always control my imagination, and the bloody moon had dipped into my fantasies.

Then beyond my dim reflection in the window, I saw it in my mind, a single main street with five buildings, three on one side, two on the other, fronted by decaying board sidewalks and derelict hitching posts: the town, stark and spare as a movie set. Strange flowers grew there as well, and some creature that I could not identify, cast a low and moving shadow on the sides of the buildings. Far to the east, flooding the gray buildings with bloody light, floated the misshapen moon. On the skyline, a horse and rider galloped the horizon, black against red. A hero always gallops along the horizon, you know. I could not see the rider's face, so I gave him the face of the boy I loved. I might have been dreaming.

Dust blew along the edge of the imaginary world and hid them all. Strange what one remembers over the space of years.

After a time, the moon lifted, turning pink, going pale as it rose into the night sky, a tarnished coin nibbled by rats.

The ghost town, or ghost of a town, was gone in a breath. The moon climbed high into the sky, all made of silver now, bright and clean. It was just the moon. Uneasily and by degrees, I settled against my window and at last fell asleep.

When the bus rolled gently to a stop at the high school, the moon was tiny, westering, pale, soon to be sinking to its death behind the mountain. If the other girls had seen the blood moon, they did not speak of it.

The ghost town exists only in my imagination, but its memory lingers still. The ghost town was as real to me then as was the song about the band of gold.

We made it back to town. One by one, the girls gathered their things and walked away from the bus into the chill September night.

We grew up, we worked, we went to college, we fell in and out of love, we married, we had children, and we did any number of things that women do. For some of us love never came. Others have worn the band of gold so long that ring fingers bear deeply incised grooves. For some, the dream lived and lives still. For others, dreams turned to dust, and, well-watered by tears, sprang up once more, green and fresh. For some, like me, love came late, unlooked for. And for some, hope withered and blew itself away.

The boy I dreamed of as I rode that dark bus is dead now,

gone too soon. One of the girls perished in a car crash a long time ago. Of most others, I know nothing; they are lost to me.

But at times in the night when someone else is driving, when I am flying in an airliner, when I am riding on a bus, and I grow sleepy—once in a while I seem to hear sweet voices from far away. The voices are singing *Band of Gold*, the sound falling from the ether like a silken scarf settling after having been tossed from a great height. And then I open an eye to see if there is blood on the moon.

I think of the bus girls then, and I see my imagined ghost town, but only from a distance. Still, it is hard-edged and black against a reddened sky, a place of hard, desert dreams. Then I look down at my hands and see the band of gold. In the night, in the far darkness of years, I rub the ring with my finger, and it shines.

Up Lake Creek

Winters are harsh at 6,000 feet. When I was in high school, for several winters we kept our horses up Lake Creek on a large acreage owned by George Castle, who was often away mining in the southwest during the winter. If we took care of George's horses, we could keep our two, Tony and Shag, on the Lake Creek place along with his.

George's Lake Creek ranch consisted of a shed, a large field in alfalfa, a huge potato cellar half-buried in the ground, and a 40-acre pasture. The winter hay for the horses was kept in the potato cellar. If the hay had not been behind closed doors, the local elk would have eaten it all in no time.

However, because the hay was stored in the potato cellar, two or three times a week someone had to get to Lake Creek, snowshoe half a mile in from the road, and drag out several bales for the horses. There was a house just off the highway at the entrance to Lake Creek Canyon, and the owner was kind enough to let us park off the road in the plowed driveway while we made the trek upcanyon to the potato cellar because, of course, then no one lived up Lake Creek, and in the winter the small road to George's ranch was not plowed.

During the week, Dad would make this journey in the dark, before he came home from work. I now wonder that he never complained, even though he left the house for work before dawn, and the darkness and winter-night cold would fill

Looking down into Lake Creek Canyon from
the east ridge in the late fall, 1960.

Lake Creek before he ever left Sun Valley to hike in to feed the horses. It was one of those things I took for granted; he didn't want me to have to do it in the dark and on a school night, for night comes early in the winter, and although I got out of school two hours before Dad came home from work, it would have been fully dark before I could have reached the potato cellar.

On Saturdays, however, this task would be mine. I didn't mind. I looked forward to seeing the horses and to feeding each of them an apple, a carrot, or a handful of oats. No one would be up Lake Creek Canyon but me, and after a week of being confined by the snow and cold to indoor rooms full of people, this was a good thing. I'd pack a thermos of coffee, make myself a sandwich, grab some horse treats from the fridge, load up a book, my camera and snowshoes, and drive our pickup the five miles from our house to the parking spot off the road at the entrance to Lake Creek Canyon.

Then I would lash on my long, narrow snowshoes and grab the bag. I'd kick myself to the top of the snowbank and onto the surface on the snow and be on my way, to spend the day with the horses, driving myself home at the end of the afternoon.

Once in a while, the pickup would be needed by someone else in the family during the day, so Dad would take an early lunch hour, drive home to get me, and drop me off at the Lake Creek parking space. Mom was working on the mountain in those days. I have no idea what her job title was, but she would leave our house in the early darkness and ride the ski lift up to the Roundhouse, a large building three-fourths of the way to the top of Bald Mountain, where, with several other women she would make soup, hot chocolate, and sandwiches, serve them to hungry skiers, clean up the building, and at the end of her day, put on her skis and ski down the mountain to the parking lot below. Mom was an expert skier.

The ski lift and the Roundhouse closed in the late afternoon when the ski runs were in shadow, so she would come off the mountain well before dark. Since Dad often worked until after dark, it would be Mom who drove out to Lake Creek to pick me up on the days when I didn't have the pickup. Mom's and Dad's days off, as is usual for those who work for a resort, were not weekend days. Often, Dad would go an entire season, and sometimes an entire year, without a day off.

This particular day was a Saturday in mid-January, a cloudy day threatening snow, so it was warmer than usual, only a few degrees below freezing. Because it was warm, instead of my heavy boots, I put on my cowboy boots to wear up Lake Creek. Dad swooped down from work and ferried me to Lake Creek at about eleven a.m. Mom was to pick me up in the late afternoon.

I strapped on the snowshoes, grabbed my bag, and realized that I had forgotten to bring my camera. "Oh, well," I thought, waving goodbye to Dad. "I've got lots of pictures of the horses. I won't need a camera today." I climbed up the steep snowbank to the surface of the snow and set out upcanyon.

The distance from the parking spot to the potato cellar on George's property was just a little less than half a mile, all of it uphill. The snow lay deep and even over the invisible dirt road.

I took my time. The gray clouds lowered until they hid the tops of the near hills. To the west, the sheep trail, fifty yards wide, showed only the dark tops of its fenceposts. I knew that by now all the sheep had been trailed to the lower country and were getting ready for lambing.

To the east stretched George Castle's alfalfa field, now peacefully blanketed in unmarked white, the year's hay stacked in the potato cellar by me and our friend Whiskey Chamberlain during a few hot, itchy August days. Farther to the east, immediately beyond the field, rose steep, unnamed hills cut by gullies and graced near their feet with groves of aspens, now stark and bare.

The cowboy boots had been a mistake, I thought as I crested

the long hill. My feet were already getting cold.

The horses came to the gate with loud whinnies and much vigorous nodding of heads. Buried in snow, the gate was not openable. Instead, I climbed over the fence with care; only the top strand of barbed wire was visible above the snow. On the pasture side, the five horses had trampled the snow down so far that I half-fell at their feet in a tangle of snowshoes and bag. They nosed at me.

The horses—Rudy, Nellie, Bonnie, Tony, and Shag—knew what I had brought, and after I stripped off the snowshoes and stood them upright in the snow, I faced a half-circle of curious faces, soft nostrils, and a chorus of breathy *huh-huh-huhs*. I reached into my bag and spent ten minutes doling out apple halves, carrots, and sugar cubes.

Then I removed the heavy chain that held them together and tugged open the huge doors of the potato cellar, diving into the black interior and dragging out bale after bale of hay, enough to last the horses until Tuesday night, when Dad would snowshoe in after dark to feed them again.

The work of the day finished, it was time for lunch. I pulled a hay bale over to one of the two concrete wing walls that made a sheltered courtyard of the entrance to the potato cellar, sat on the bale, drew up my cold feet, and leaned back against the cement. I had a rather lavish lunch that day: hot split pea soup from a thermos, a tuna sandwich, and two chocolate chip cookies. This was the life, I told myself as steam from the soup clouded my glasses. The horses began to tear into the hay, and the only sound in the world was the rhythmic grinding of their jaws.

Far across the field, something moved on the hillside. A line of about twenty elk forged a horizontal path through the snow, heading southeast toward Wood River. I hadn't noticed them before. Walking uphill on snowshoes, it's best to watch one's snowshoes, and, of course, I had just been occupied with the horses and the hay.

The elk moved across the hillside slowly, taking turns break-ing trail in the shoulder-deep snow. By the time I had finished my lunch, they had made about two hundred yards and were bedding down in one of the aspen groves.

Suddenly I felt an icy wind from the southeast, and I decid-ed to take my book and flashlight and go indoors to read for a while. The cold would follow me inside, but I could make myself a little cubbyhole in the hay bales to warm myself while I read the afternoon away. I looked at my watch. Two-thirty. Mom was to pick me up at four.

Hoping for another treat, my own horse, Tony, followed me into the dark potato cellar. Without warning, Tony shied violently backward and bolted from the cellar. Lying at my feet was a coyote.

I stood as if paralyzed. It took me a long moment to realize that the coyote was dead, frozen stiff. I dug into my bag for the flashlight.

The light glinted sharply from the coyote's bared teeth. Curious, I examined the dead coyote. The coyote was a male. His coat was glossy and winter-prime, and he had not starved to death, nor had he been shot. I wondered if he had encoun-tered a 10-80 cyanide trap, but there was no way to tell. How had the coyote managed to get inside the potato cellar? That was a mystery, too.

Stepping around the coyote, I sent my flashlight beam into the far gloom of the potato cellar, following a narrow pathway on the damp dirt floor between massed stacks of bales until I had nearly reached the earthen wall at the back. The air felt dead, cold as a tomb. I moved a few bales to create a sitting nook, and wormed myself in, pulling the bales close around me and tucking my feet up. I tugged my hat down over my ears and re-set the wool scarf around my neck and chin.

The flashlight I jammed into the hay at just the right angle before I retrieved my book from the bag. Today's book was one of the paperbacks that Dad had found abandoned on a ski bus. He often found such books on the ski buses. Lost books, scarves, mittens, hats, ski goggles, and the like would sit in a wooden box beside his desk for several weeks before Dad or his bus drivers would bring the unclaimed items home. Our family never wanted for hats and mittens, and I was always eager for the books.

I sighed and settled myself comfortably into the hay. Fritz Leiber was the author of today's prize. I knew what to expect from Fritz Leiber, and I smiled as I inhaled the sweet smell of alfalfa hay and entered the strange world of *Fahfrd and the Grey Mouser*.

Time passed and outside the potato cellar, the wind was rising. My nook in the hay felt warm and cozy, if cramped. I put a mittened hand over my nose to warm it and looked toward the open doors of the cellar. The light had changed. I could see a ragged patch of blue over the east ridge. That wind was tearing at the clouds, blowing them away. The air felt colder.

I hunched further into my niche and readjusted the flashlight. It was dark in Fahfrd's world. He was padding down an alley, hoping to disappear. But I couldn't follow him. Something inside the potato cellar, something besides me, was breathing.

Through the open doors, I could see portions of all five horses feasting on the hay I had set out: sorrels Rudy and Bonnie, dark-bay Shag, black Nellie, and Tony, dapple gray. The breathing in the potato cellar was rapid, shallow, and *close*. It was not the horses.

I dog-eared the page and shut my book quietly, grabbing the flashlight as I got to my feet. My legs had gone to sleep; I stood for a few moments, swaying, waiting for the pins and needles to subside. I could hear the breathing still, and finally began to move toward it, my flashlight beam splatted on the back wall of brown dirt. Could this be another coyote, sick or rabid, crouching in the dark behind the last of the bales?

White things. There were white things, rounded and in a row, strung along the top of the dirt wall, on the narrow shelf where that wall met the metal base supporting the potato cellar's roof. The white things moved. I shone my flashlight there and was startled by eyeshine.

I nearly dropped the flashlight in relief. The rounded white things were rabbits.

They looked at me, six of them, turning their heads toward the light. I expected them to scatter madly away in fear. But the white rabbits stayed in place, a twitch of a black-tipped ear and the chewing rhythm of a whiskery muzzle the only things that moved.

The sweet hay in the cellar had no doubt attracted them, and they had most likely entered in the same way that the coyote had done.

I stepped closer and closer, and still the rabbits did not move. I stacked two hay bales against the wall, climbed up, and found myself eye to eye with one of them.

The creatures showed no fear. The clear amber eyes seemed to look right through me. I could not resist touching them, and put my hand out to each one, petting the cloud-soft fur, examining the huge hind feet, and smoothing a finger along the velvety muzzles.

I felt odd, as if I had entered some cold and forgotten temple and the gods there had little regard for this world but were focused solely on another. At least, in the potato cellar, there was no shortage of offering.

Shivering, I backed away, climbed down from the bales, and watched them, fascinated. By then I knew that they were not rabbits, of course. They were snowshoe hares, those nimble and secretive fellows that wear coats of brown all summer and change into white robes when the snows come. The snowshoes didn't move, didn't turn their heads to look at me.

Eventually, I realized that the light outside had faded, and so had the beam of my flashlight. It was after five. Hurriedly, I chained shut the great doors, patted the horses good-bye, tossed my snowshoes over the gate, and climbed over the fence after them. I strapped my cowboy boots into the snowshoes and made tracks down the long hill.

Twilight was well on the way to darkness. I hoped Mom wouldn't be irritated if I was late in getting to the parking spot. I knew she had left the house in the dark of the morning, in the coldest part of the night, and, with her skis and poles, had ridden the ski lift up Bald Mountain to the Roundhouse. After the Roundhouse and the ski lift closed for the day, she would ski down to her car. She'd be tired and anxious to get home. I tried to hurry.

Wearing the flimsy cowboy boots, my feet were already uncomfortably cold. The kindly cloud cover that had held in the meager heat of the day, had been swept away by the wind. "I think it's about twenty below," I thought. "That's not bad for January." Indeed, it was usual.

In the deepening twilight, I located the aspen grove where the elk had been resting. They had gone. No lights starred my field of view. The lone house was at the bottom of the hill where the parking place had been plowed? That house was dark. I rushed on, making a conscious effort to keep my balance at the increased pace.

Darkness fitted to the canyon like a black glove. Above, the moonless sky filled with the sweeping, cloudy arc of the Milky Way. I had to break out the flashlight to find my path for the final hundred yards.

When I reached the parking place, it was empty. After five, and no Mom. She had never been late before. "She'll come," I thought. "She always does." I took off the snowshoes and stomped around on the flattened snow for some time in an attempt to keep warm. No cars passed on the highway. I had been told many times not to walk home from Lake Creek in the winter, though the distance was no more than five miles. There was nowhere to walk except on the road, which was often ice-coated; there were many places where it would be hazardous even to walk with snowshoes on the deep snow beside the road. "I don't trust everybody," Dad had said, "and if someone you don't know stops for you, you can't run in four feet of snow. Also, not everyone is a good winter driver. You could be hit by a car. And if you try to walk on the snow, you could break through into one of those ponds."

My feet were numb. Standing on snow in cowboy boots was not good. I cast the weak beam of the flashlight around and found a cluster of small willows nearby, each one short and sprouting dozens of small trunks from the deep snow. With considerable difficulty, I climbed into one of these and, sitting two feet above the snow, arranged my scarf so that only my eyes were exposed. I shoved my hands deep into my pockets and waited.

And waited. Six. Six-thirty. Seven. The icy wind returned to the canyon.

Something was wrong. But at least here in the willow, it was getting warmer. The wind sliced through the branches around me. I could hear it moaning in the trees above the river on the far side of the highway, but I couldn't feel its chill. In fact, I felt comfortable at last. The air must be warming; a warm front must be traveling through on that wind.

Suddenly I stiffened, flailed my arms, and nearly lost my perch. "You idiot!" I said aloud. "*White Fang. The Call of the Wild. To Build a Fire.* This is what Jack London says happens to people who are about to freeze. You feel warm. You feel sleepy." I had been out and about many times on nights much colder than this one, but on those nights, I had been climbing up to a ridge to catch the moonlight, or snowshoeing along a fence not far from our house or walking home from Judy's house—not sitting still in the middle of a willow. "Idiot!" I said again.

Trying to extricate myself from the nest of branches, I fell from the willow into the snow, picked myself up, and trudged to the parking place to recover my snowshoes.

I would have to walk home. Even if the flashlight failed on the way, as it undoubtedly would, the highway, with the tall snowbanks on either side, would guide me. If a car came, I would just have to climb out of the plowed path *fast* and bail over the high banks into the snow. I slid on a patch of ice. "Damned slick cowboy boots," I muttered.

As I began walking toward the road from the parking place, I saw headlights approaching, and stopped in my tracks. Could this be Mom at last? Or perhaps it was the owner of the darkened house coming home after some event in town.

A familiar pickup turned off the highway and blinded me with its lights.

"Dad!" I thought in relief.

Dad pushed open the passenger-side door. "Are you all right?" he demanded. "Get in," he continued without waiting for an answer.

I dropped the snowshoes into the bed and climbed inside. The heat in the cab was blowing full blast, and I stripped off my mittens at once, holding my hands out to the vent. Dad was already turning around, heading back toward the highway. "Where's Mom?" I asked.

We were on the highway, gathering speed. "In the hospital," he said.

"What?" I cried, shocked. "What?" White snowbanks blurred past on both sides, and ice glittered on the road ahead.

"She's going to be all right," he said more gently, but his voice was tight and his foot heavy on the accelerator.

"What happened?" I unwound my scarf and pulled off my hat. My feet were nonexistent. I couldn't feel them at all.

"Bernice was skiing down the mountain, and some fool was

skiing too fast, lost control, and smacked right into her. She was unconscious for four hours." He glanced at me and then grinned, his teeth white in the glow from the instrument panel. "We were all there in her room," he said. "Me, your grandma, Gramps, and Vicki. The first thing she said when she woke up was 'Where's Danny?' She sent me right out to get you. That's when we knew she would be all right."

"Gosh," I whispered. "Gosh."

"She's got something wrong with one ankle," he went on, "but Dr. Saviers thinks it's just a bad sprain. She has a concussion, so they're keeping her overnight at the hospital."

Dad had reached Saddle Road, and turned left instead of continuing straight into town. "Is that where we're going?" I asked. "Isn't it after visiting hours?"

"Mom told Dr. Saviers that she wouldn't sleep until she saw your face," Dad told me. "We're going."

"I've got a story for her," I said.

"You and your stories." Dad began to whistle.

The Silk Road

It was the end of pheasant-hunting season in Idaho. In Ketchum, everything was gray and brown, even the fallen aspen leaves. Winter was coming in, and fast, as it always did in late October when I was a girl.

Dad hadn't gone hunting very often that year, for some reason. I cannot remember just why. For decades, pheasant hunting had been a passion with him, and he was good at it. Very. Exceedingly. He had guided many clients pheasant hunting over the years. Having grown up in Shoshone, he knew the "lower country" well, from Shook's Corner to Picabo, from Notch Butte to Dietrich, all the farmland and weedy irrigation ditches, all the dirt roads and pastures, all the cornfields and frost-discouraged alfalfa fields.

He was an excellent shot, and we always had pheasant, chukar, and duck in our locker in Hailey, along with venison, elk meat, and trout, to help us get by in the winter. In those days the only freezers most people had were the tiny "two-ice-cube-trays-and quart-of-ice-cream" freezers in the tops of their refrigerators. Most families in our town rented a locker in Hailey by the year, to hold their frozen game and fish, or beef and hog meat.

About once a month we would go to the locker and have the man open the big metal door. Great swooshes of frosty air would fall around our feet as we walked down the narrow hall

194

between wood-framed bins made of hardware cloth, until at last we reached the one marked "Stewart." Dad would choose white-paper-wrapped parcels marked "elkburger," "two pheasant," and maybe one on which I had proudly written "brookies." Then the man would shut the heavy door behind us and we would drive the twelve miles home from Hailey in the dark, anticipating dinners of pheasant in mushroom cream sauce, fat elkburgers topped with crisp bacon, or brook trout fried in butter.

I grew up cleaning fish and game. Dad guided, and when I was very little he would bring me feathers from some of the game birds. I wore pheasant tail feathers as a wild Indian skulking around the corral with a weak bow and arrow I had made from willow twigs. Always at Thanksgiving time, with crayons I would draw a turkey head and neck on heavy paper, cut it out, make a little slit in one end of a potato, and slide in the paper head. Then I would complete the potato turkey by sticking the potato with the gleaming iridescent blue-green speculum feathers of mallards and blue-winged teal to make wings and a fanned tail.

By the time I was eight, I was old enough to do more than play with feathers. When Dad came home tired from a day of guiding, I would clean the fish or birds and help with deer and elk.

Often, he would come in with a string of ducks and say something like this: "Barbara Stanwyck shot these, and she is having some friends to dinner at the Alpine Restaurant tonight, so you had better hustle and get these cleaned." Or I would clean a limit of pheasants shot by Clark Gable, or pintails Gary Cooper had bagged, or some goldeneye harvested by Robert Taylor. Sitting in the kitchen over a bucket, cleaning the birds, I would imag-ine the dinners where they would be served. The cook at the Alpine would boil up a huge pot of wild rice, I imagined, and he would stuff the ducks with something strange and exotic and wrap them in bacon. Then he would pop them into the oven ten at a time, roasting them to a deep gravy-brown while the whole restaurant filled with the aroma of duck and bacon. Resting on a bed of fluffy wild rice, the bacon-wrapped ducks would be brought to the table, I thought, on a silver platter surrounded with parsley. Mother roasted duck like that sometimes (minus the exotic stuffing, platter, and parsley), but we could rarely afford wild rice to go with them. As the intestines plopped into the bucket, I would think about the movie stars sitting at a long table flashing their diamonds or expensive watches and laughing with beautiful white teeth over their dinner of wild game.

Things were a little different now, however. Dad had been promoted in Sun Valley Company. He no longer had as much time to moonlight as a guide, and only did so for old-friend clients. I was seventeen and spent more of my fall weekend afternoons reading and writing and roaming the hills for wildflowers and agates, and fewer of them cleaning pheasant and duck.

This particular fall, Dad had gone hunting only once or twice. Now it was Sunday, the last day of pheasant hunting season, and Dad decided suddenly that he was going pheasant hunting. I was the only one around, and he announced that if I could be ready to go in five minutes, I could go with him. I loved going with Dad simply because of being with him, but also because for me every trip was and has always been a quest for a story.

We got into the little blue Rambler American and headed south through Hailey into the lower country. The trees in Ketchum were already bare, but at the lower elevations, tattered leaves still clung to cottonwoods and the tamer trees of the farmsteads. Everything was fading back into the earth, and although the sun was bright and the sky a brilliant blue, there was a sense of letting go. November felt just around the corner, as if it had its fingers on the doorjamb.

By the time we reached the Dietrich country, the afternoon

was old. The sun was well on its way toward the western fields. We drove up and down and across the sparse lattice of old dirt farm roads, scarcely meeting a vehicle of any kind.

I felt that the place was old, past its prime. There were farmhouses scattered here and there, but none of them had been built during my lifetime. Many were abandoned and leaning. Most of the barns, doorless and weathered gray, had not housed livestock for decades. The farms that were still being worked were for the most part the property of absentee owners, not those who lived on their own lands. Nevertheless, these farms were not the "new agriculture," this meaning concrete-lined irrigation ditches, clean-to-the-ground harvesting, and no weeds to be seen. These were pheasant-friendly "old agriculture" farms, where wild grasses and weeds grew tall on the margins of the ditches, and where stubblefields promised winter food and cover for pheasants, ducks, geese, quail, rabbits, deer, and other wild creatures.

Insulated from the sharp wind by the window glass of the Rambler, I looked out at the sunny fields passing with a kind of strange regret that I had not seen them when the houses were bright with new paint and the yards neatly kept or scattered with children's toys, when saddle horses stood sleek in the corrals, when driveways held clean and polished cars, and when fresh curtains were hung in all the windows. This land must have some stories, I thought in distress, but I cannot find them, and all the people who could tell those stories have died or gone away.

Dad would park half in the barrow pit at a promising place along a road, take out his shotgun, and walk a field. I would wait until I could see him back on the road and waving, and then, proud of my rarely used driver's license, would drive the Rambler to pick him up. He, however, would drive to the next promising spot.

The sun sank farther and farther to the west. Dad had

My father, Clayton Stewart,
pheasant hunting near Shoshone.

four pheasants now, all beautiful bronze roosters with the green-frosted flanks and red faces that I knew so well, having cleaned so many over the years. This was a good day, as five pheasants was the legal limit.

The blue of the sky began to grow pearly and pale. A cottony fuzziness edged the horizon all around. "That's fog coming in," Dad said. "I need one more rooster to limit out. That fog is going to be here in half an hour, or at least it will be high enough to cover up the sun. Let's move. I know a place along the railroad tracks where there's a ditch and cattails next to some fields where there isn't a house for miles. I'll bet I can scare up one more pheasant there. It's a place where I used to take clients who hadn't bagged a thing all day." He turned down a small gravel road and then down a smaller dirt road.

Railroad tracks paralleled the road on the east. Sure enough, next to the tracks lay a marshy ditch bristling with cattails. On the west side of the road I saw the inevitable barbed-wire fence, some of its wooden posts leaning this way and that. Close inside the fence ran a line of heavy old-fashioned telephone poles, the kind with two wooden crossbars and big glass insulators. On the other side of the fence was a field of corn and corn stubble. Some of the corn had not been cut and stood taller than a man could reach, field corn destined for livestock feed. This was a perfect place for pheasants.

"I'm going to take off into that uncut patch," Dad said, shouldering his shotgun while a blast of cold air blew in through the open car door. "I'm going to circle around and come back here, so this time you don't have to watch for me to wave." The car door shut with a hollow *chunk*, and Dad strode off into the corn.

To the west, the wall of fog loomed higher, and it was closer. The sun began to descend into the fog, and I was glad it was Dad out there in the corn and not me, because I knew he never got lost.

This time, Dad was gone for a long time. Once I heard his

shotgun pop. He was somewhere on the far side of the stand of uncut corn.

I always carried a book. I got out my book and soon was lost in its little world. I floated weightless in black space, Heinlein space, far from cornfields, dilapidated farmhouses, railroad tracks, barbed-wire fences, and old-fashioned telephone poles.

I glanced up. The fog had receded, now only a blur on the western horizon. Far down the dirt road, Dad was walking back to the car, shotgun over his shoulder. He was carrying something. I shut my book and slid to the driver's seat, preparing to start the car and drive to him.

Then I saw the webs. The sun was a fuzzy orange ball, falling into the fog on the western horizon. Its slanting rays cast long shadows from telephone poles and fenceposts, and from the corn and wild roadside grasses. But that was not all the sun showed me. The world was draped in silvery strands held horizontal by a slight breeze. They were cobwebs.

Cobwebs draped every line of barbed wire, waved gently from every cornstalk, every blade of grass, and made a strangeness of the telephone poles.

I knew that in the autumn, baby spiders disperse to new territories. When he is ready to travel, a spiderling climbs to the top of something—a grass blade, a twig, a post—and, spinning a long thread and using it as a parachute, the little fellow lets the wind take him. Often, many spiderlings will choose the same, perfect, breezy fall day to travel. In years past, I remembered fall days when spider silk caught the sun here and there along trails at home where I rode my horse.

But not like this. The ground was netted over with spun silver, layer upon layer, like a fleece blanket. All the barbed wires, line after line, were hung with silk strands, as well as the fenceposts. As the sun sank lower and lower, the telephone poles were the strangest of all. The telephone poles, with their old double crossbars, carried so many strands of silk that they looked draped with fabric.

The telephone poles were shrouded in filaments that trailed twenty feet from the poles and crossbars, like the tattered sails of a great ghost ship. There was so much silk hanging from the poles that it seemed they must crack and fall from the sheer weight of all the threads. But of course, the spider silk was as light as—cobweb.

The spider silk turned orange as the sun went down, and all the world was covered in ragged, shimmering silk. The light fled, gleaming down the threads as they lifted and fell with the small wind passing over the cornfield. How many spiderlings could there be in an Idaho cornfield? How many tiny voyagers had launched themselves toward new lives and left their lifelines shining where the wind had taken them? How many spiders lived in the world I thought I knew?

Only the tip of the sun's disk could still be seen above the fog to the west. Dad came up to the car and hauled the door open as I slid over to the passenger seat. He slung his pheasant onto the floor in the back seat with the other four. "That's the limit," he said, shutting the car door.

I gasped. "I'm sorry I didn't drive down to get you," I said. The spiderwebs—" I didn't know how to say it.

"That's all right," he said, his hand on the ignition key but not turning it. "I see them, too. It doesn't happen very often that you see all the threads. My dad and I would see them once in a great while when we were hunting this country, if the sun was just right. But in those days there were not so many. I have never seen them like this."

For a long moment we stared at the strange mastlike telephone poles lifting their burden of rotted sails, the long lines of barbed wire streaming with web, the grasses and the corn flexing as the wind fingered the strands, long light flowing along them like mercury.

Then the sun was gone, and in that instant, the world of the spiders vanished. "Like magic" is the trite phrase that comes to mind. But the spiderweb was gone in the blink of an eye with the passing of the sunlight.

Dad turned the key and pulled out onto the dirt road. Gradually the Rambler gained momentum. The fog began to close in once more as the light faded. Twilight deepens swiftly in late autumn.

Abandoned farmhouses gaped as they loomed in the mist, and I knew that the people had cast their fortunes elsewhere, like the tiny spiders, and had been carried away.

I had been looking in the wrong place for the stories these fields had to tell. The stories of these old fields and farmsteads were not human stories, but spider stories. When the people went away, it was left to the spiders to tell tales of leaning doors and eyeless windows; of buzzing flies and dusty floors and fading wallpaper; of abandoned fields, or fields seldom visited; of weedy gardens, dying lawns, and dead trees. The spiders had spun their tales in all these places, myth and legend for us to find and to read, if we could.

Today's tale was the story of invisible travelers on the silk road, of tall corn and tall grasses, tall fence posts, and highest and best, the telephone poles rearing their tattered heads into the sky, together a great unending ship of passage. The place looked like farmland. When the sun was high, the place had looked like a domesticated landscape that people had made their own, but the slanting sunlight had shown us that this was not a place for people, not any more. The spiders lived here now, and all the stories were their stories.

Safe

One thing is certain and the rest is lies;
The Flower that once has blown for ever dies.
— Omar Khayyam, the Rubaiyat

After work, my dad was a prospector, and what he liked best to find was gold. We panned, we dug, we chipped pieces of stone and sent them off for assay, and yes, we found some gold. But that is another story.

Dad also loved tales of treasure, especially gold treasure, and this was one of his favorites. He would tell me the story that I came to think of as "The Lost Safe of Shoshone" over and over as we drove somewhere, anywhere—to go fishing, or on a foray to look at new cars, or simply for a short ride to fill the water tanks for the horses pastured at Lake Creek.

"It was this way, Danny," he would say, his intense brown eyes fixed on the road ahead and his big hands firmly gripping the steering wheel of our 1949 Jeep, "There was a place in Utah where gold, a lot of gold, was kept in a safe. I think the gold was in bars, but it might have been in gold coins. This was in the 1880s or 1890s, I think. And some men broke out of the Utah State Penitentiary and knew about the gold in this safe, and they figured that if they took the gold and could go north and get it across the border into Canada, they would be made men. So they stole a team of horses and a heavy wagon, and then stole the safe, and took off north. They couldn't open the safe or didn't have time to try, so they just got the thing into the stolen wagon somehow and took off for Idaho on their way to Canada.

"But by then a posse was hot on their trail. The outlaws kept going as fast as those horses could go, and eventually found themselves in the dark with the posse close behind, in a lava field north of Shoshone, going like hell over the rocks with the wagon bouncing to pieces and the horses running with their last strength. But the posse caught up to the men and captured them before sunup. They got the wagon and the horses, too, but they didn't get the gold." Here Dad would smile a tight little smile. "By the time the posse found the men, the safe was gone."

"What happened to the gold, Dad?" I would ask every time he told the story.

"It's out there, Danny," he would say. "The escaped prisoners were taken back to the Utah State Pen, where they were questioned about the gold, but they never told what they had done with the safe just before they were captured. It was dark, see, and they took that safe from the wagon—or maybe it fell off—and they hid it because they knew the posse was close, and then they climbed back into the wagon and kept going, just ahead of the posse, maybe leading the posse away from where they had ditched the safe, until they were captured. That safe with all its gold?" His eyes would get a little dreamy here, and he would squint as if shutting out the view of the road and seeing the gold in his mind. I knew better than to answer his question. He always answered it himself.

"That safe is out there in the lava desert, somewhere north of Shoshone," Dad would always say. "I figure it's west of the highway, because of something Gramps once said. And I bet even those prisoners themselves couldn't have located it again if they had tried. Oh, the posse looked for it. And looked for it and looked for it, because that was a lot of gold. And a number

of people since have looked for it. But no one has ever found it."
His voice would soften just a little, and he'd finish the story by
saying, "You know how much gold was in that safe?"

"No," I would always say. "How much?"

"Four million dollars," he would reply. "Four million dollars
at today's price of gold, thirty-two dollars an ounce. Think of
it. Four million dollars out there in the sagebrush somewhere,
in that old safe, out in the lava." Dad would shake his head;
the story would always end there. After all these years, I have
to laugh. With inflation, that gold would now be worth about
eighty million dollars.

Several times while I was growing up, we went to look for
the safe, usually in late winter, when our home town had been
choked with snow for many weeks and we were feeling the
stirrings of cabin fever.

Mom would pack a picnic lunch, and we would head to the
lower country where the snow had already melted into spring.
Sometimes we would go to the trout farm for the picnic. Some-
times we would go to the arrowhead-finding place near King
Hill. Sometimes we would picnic in a green pasture down in the
Snake River Canyon near Hagerman.

And every few years we would go out into the lava desert
northwest of Shoshone to have our picnic. We'd walk on and
around the edges of the black basalt flow with its scrubby bushes, tender spring flowers, and sparse grasses, and we'd look for
the old safe and its gold. Once in a while Dad would take off on
a Saturday afternoon and look for the gold by himself.

But none of us ever found the stolen gold. Whenever we drove
to Twin Falls or Shoshone, I would sit with my face pressed
to the car window as we drove past that black and jagged lava
flow. Even as a child I could see that the lava was more than
a match for a horse-drawn wagon, especially in the dark. And
I would daydream about four million dollars' worth of gold.
I don't remember that I dreamed about what the gold would

buy, just of the gold itself. Would the gold be bars, heavy and dense? Would the safe be filled instead with gray canvas bags of gold coins? Or would the bright coins be loose inside the safe, mounds and mounds of them? That would be best. Coins. Indianheads and eagles, beautiful, bright, shining, *mine*.

A few short years later, I was finding it very difficult to be a teen. Now, decades past, I know that many, if not most teens feel that way, but I didn't know that when I was seventeen. I was odd then, a little strange, and couldn't bring myself to do much fitting in, or simply *could not* fit in, so I was sometimes lonely—but not lonely enough to change. I am still odd, but now my world is wider, and I have found not many, but at least several friends who can tolerate my strangeness and who accept me. I had few friends then, none very close.

I found solace on an unusual path: the study of wildflowers. All spring and summer, and until the killing frosts in the fall, I roamed the hills of home, looking for wildflowers, trying to identify them, sketching them, taking notes on when and where they grew and bloomed, and collecting their seeds for planting in my small garden. I was not popular—or even much noticed—at school, but when I was on my own, I was wildflower girl. That alone made me strange; I discovered that although we were at school to learn, few wanted to associate with someone who knew things. It was considered elitist to know things, and especially undesirable to strive to learn more on one's own. Life would have been much easier for me as a teen if instead of wildflowers, I had bent my efforts toward fashion, hair styling, sports, popular songs, the latest dance craze, flirting, and makeup application techniques. But, driven by some inner vision, I knew that none of those things were me, wildflower girl.

Winters are long and harsh at 6,000 feet, and those winters meant snow and ice, deep snow for months, and no wildflowers. Winters were difficult for me. I buried myself in books and went out into the night and up into the hills alone in the cold darkness to learn the stars when my classmates were dancing, or going to the movies, or trying on clothes in their best friends' bedrooms, or snugged into cozy booths at a local drive-in with hamburgers and milkshakes and their dates. Every year, I waited impatiently for spring, for snowmelt, when the wildflowers would come out once more.

Wildflower girl was foolish. Didn't she know that dances were more important? And talking on the phone to friends? Shopping for clothes? Trying out makeup? Or didn't she care?

I did care about the typical concerns of teenage girls. I just did not care enough. I didn't know it then, but wildflowers were to become my career and my life. Only a few short years later, I would be out under the open sky, concerned with wild plants and flowers, almost every day for tens and tens of years.

One cold and bright April afternoon of my senior year in high school, a day when the snow was melting away from the roads but still holding stubbornly to the hillsides, I was astonished to see pulled up in our driveway an old black car containing three teenagers. There was Millie, one of my few real friends, who had been my friend since the first grade. The second person was her easygoing brother Paul, and in the back seat I spied another senior, Ralph. I was surprised to see Ralph there.

"Hey," said Paul, who was driving. "We're going down to the lower country this afternoon. Want to come?"

Want to come? This was not a question anyone my age had asked me for years. And in the lower country, it would truly be spring and there would be wildflowers. Of course, I wanted to come!

Ralph was a newcomer to our high school, and he and I had formed a tentative friendship not many months before this. He was a bright, intense, tightly wound boy, curious about the world, witty and kind. We would sometimes call each other after school and meet long after dark to talk about things teens talk about—the world, good and evil, school, and the future.

After we had talked, Ralph would always be the first to leave. When Ralph stood to go, he would say something to this effect: "I'm not a good person. I wish you knew. I wish I could make you understand. But deep down, I am evil, I am rotten inside." And I would say, "You aren't evil. I can't imagine why you think you are evil." And truly, I couldn't imagine it. Ralph was not perfect, but he was considerate and honest. I had never seen him do anything mean or devious. And I had no fear at all of meeting him at midnight in a deserted place.

Ralph would melt into the darkness and I would listen to his footsteps fading in the night and the sound of his car pulling away before I set out for home myself. I wondered what had happened in his life, what he had thought or done, to make him feel that he was evil, and how I might convince him that he was not.

Before many of these meetings had taken place, I discovered that Ralph and I were much alike. He was an unusual person, different, too bright, too intense. And he wanted desperately to fit into the rigid, unforgiving social structure of our high school, to be respected, to have scores of laughing friends, to be included in many activities, to be accepted, and above all, to be safe from ridicule. Ralph told me many times how he hoped to discipline himself to change, to fit in, to be highly desirable to the "in" crowd, to become popular, to become good. And to be safe.

We discussed strategies for making this happen. He would report on his progress, and he was making progress. He made the track team. He asked, and a sweet, popular girl accepted a date.

But I wouldn't, or more likely, couldn't, do the same. Also, I had decided that fitting in was too high a price to pay for my differences and knew that I would continue on my strange and solitary path to what I might become, regardless of the loneliness. Ralph was on his way *in*, on his way to acceptance by the others in the high school and doing rather well at it—and I was on my way *out*. For a time we met in the middle. Then things shifted.

But on this bright, clear April day, we were simply four friends escaping from winter into spring for one magical afternoon. The town of Hailey sped by, followed by smaller Bellevue, and then the patchy farmland along Wood River slipped past. Up over Timmerman Hill, and the black car rolled down the narrow ribbon of highway into the snowless sagebrush desert, driving downhill into spring.

After twenty miles or so of desert, we came to the place where the familiar dark lava flow crossed the highway, and Paul pulled off the road and stopped. "This looks like an interesting place to walk around," he said.

We followed Paul out into the sage and black lava. The very first of the wildflowers were out and I searched for them eagerly. Yellowbells nodded in the fresh wind, and bluebells and waterleaf hid in the star moss beneath the sage. This was a fine outing for wildflower girl.

The afternoon sun shone bright and clear. We walked for some time over the rough surface of the old flow, and then we came to a water channel, a blackly weird water channel. The channel carved into the lava was very deep, thirty or forty feet deep, and perhaps only ten or twelve feet wide at the top.

The bottom of this stark slit in the world was a series of round, cauldron-like lava bowls half-filled with both quartz sand and rounded rocks ranging from marble to watermelon in size, having been whirled and whirled against the black basalt of the sandy streamed until they were polished smooth. The stones had created the lava bowls; the bowls had created the polished stones.

The others continued walking out into the desert, but for once I abandoned the quest for wildflowers. I felt drawn to this small canyon, a dark and unexpected slash in the gray, undulating world of the sagebrush desert. There was no water in the streambed when I climbed down to it; the sand there was dry. The water to come was still locked in the high country and wouldn't make its way to the desert until high-altitude snowmelt in May and June.

I climbed slowly and carefully thirty feet down the steep and slick lava walls into the bottom, and there the miniature canyon was so narrow that I could put a hand on each wall as I lowered myself into one after another of the stone bowls. The dry streambed was curvy and winding, doubling this way and that where eons of intermittent stream flow had found paths of least resistance in the lava it was wearing through.

And then I saw it below me, wedged tightly between the narrowing black stone walls: a black cuboidal hulk.

Could it be? Was it possible? Pulling myself hand over hand along the walls of the canyon, I hurried forward.

It was. A large black safe stood crookedly in one of the stone bowls, crazily canted, wedged between the two walls of the miniature canyon. I could see that its door must be on the other side. By now the canyon was so narrow that there was no room to go around. I had to climb over the safe to get to its far side.

I held my breath, fighting my rising excitement. A safe! A safe, a big safe, a honking big safe, perhaps three feet tall and wide, in the lava desert northwest of Shoshone! Could it be, could it be?

And my mind filled with all the possibilities and the sharp gleam of gold.

I scrambled over the safe. The door was open, dangling by one hinge. Eagerly I knelt to the safe, and—

The safe was full of sand—beautiful, pale, clean, sparkling quartz sand. I sat back on my heels and let out a long breath. "Wells" was written on the door in faded gilt letters, underlined with black and gold arabesques. "Well, Wells," I thought.

"Where's the gold?"

Darkness covered the desert, and before you could see them, you heard the ring of iron-rimmed wheels on stone and the ragged gasping of the horses. They clattered to a halt, and a man grunted, "Here. This will do. Come on, Mick, Aaron, Joe. Help me. They're getting close!"

And then in the dark a heave, a cry bitten off short, a curse, and the sound of something impossibly heavy cracking into the canyon walls. Once, twice, three times *smash*, and a thud when it came to rest, wedged tightly between lava walls above a rock bowl full of sand. Then from above, the snap of long reins, hooves and wheels moving, noises fading. I blinked.

"It was dark when they ditched the safe," I thought. "Dad has always told that in the story. And it's thought that they took the safe because they didn't have a chance to get it open. Otherwise, why take the heavy safe and not just the gold? So," I told myself, "the gold was in the safe when it fell into the ravine." I looked at the safe and its hanging door, at the black enamel surface with its patches of rust, at the golden arabesques painted there. "And did they come back for it when, years later, they might have been released from prison? Could they have remembered where they had ditched the safe? Or," I thought, liking this explanation best, "did the door come open when the safe crashed into the lava wall? Is the gold still here in one of these descending, stair-stepping bowls of sand? Gold is heavier than either quartz or lava." The gold would be under the sand.

I dug with both hands in the pale sand below the safe. Nothing. I moved downstream to the next lava bowl and dug in the sand there. Nothing. Undaunted, I dug in several more downstream bowls. "Maybe the safe's door came open before it came to rest where it is now," I thought. "If that's the case, the gold will be upstream." Quickly, I climbed over the safe and searched two sand-filled bowls upstream. I dug in more sand, in more bowls.

211

A voice from above broke through my concentration and I looked up at the narrow crack of sky to see Ralph's head leaning over the canyon rim. "Hey, come on up, Dana. Paul is ready to go home."

"I'll be back," I told myself, using small handholds and scrub sage to haul myself up the smooth black side of the ravine.

Paul and Millie were smiling, and Millie held a little bouquet of spring flowers. "It's been a good day," Paul said, slipping the car into gear. "We saw some meadowlarks and a lizard, and two hawks."

As we got into the back seat, Ralph handed me a small plant covered with tiny purple flowers. "Here's one we don't know," he said. I took it with care. No boy had ever given me a flower before. "It's in the pea and bean family," I said, looking closely at the bonnetlike flowers and the silvery fuzz on the stems and fernlike leaves. "I'll find out what it is."

And when I got home, I pressed the plant in the leather-bound copy of *The Rubaiyat of Omar Khayyam* that my grandmother Rowene had given me. Ralph's plant wasn't in my field guides. Our town had no bookstore, there was no internet, and the library had no western botany books, so I never could tell him its name.

Our friendship drifted a little as we neared graduation. Ralph was making great strides in his campaign to fit in. He went to the senior parties; I went alone into the hills. I would pass him smiling in the halls of our high school, laughing with other friends. The strategy we had crafted for him in our midnight talks was working. He always had a word and a smile for me, but he was well on his way *in* now, almost an insider with the popular crowd, and I was well on my way *out*.

Still, after graduation, we wrote each other often for a year or so, and then I lost him. I had gone to college. He had joined the military. I can't remember now whether it was the Army or the Marines, but the last thing he sent me was a black and white photograph of himself in uniform, head and shoulders, an official military photo.

And then my letters went unanswered. Months later they were returned "address unknown." I thought we had simply grown too far apart to be friends. Or, in truth, I felt that he now had the kind of friends he had been seeking, beautiful and popular friends much different from the likes of weird wildflower girl.

Fifty years have come and gone since that black and white photo came in the mail to the college girl I was then, the photo in which Ralph looked strangely innocent as a second lieutenant in his smart uniform topped by the officer's cap with its black and shining visor.

He had taken himself out of my life. I imagined him surrounded by comrades and friends after hours, telling stories in a bar, maybe. Or crisply handsome in dress uniform, dancing with a beautiful young woman at a military ball; or cheering at a football game, sitting with his buddies, beers in hand—places and activities that were alien to me with my hills and sagebrush, the lonely canyons, the campfires and the stars, the trees and the wildflowers.

What I did not imagine was Ralph grimy and grim, sweating in the jungles of Vietnam.

I thought of him once in a while, and of our long talks in the dark. I hoped he had carved his desired path all the way inside, inside a large circle of people who cared about him, where he would be safely accepted and would not need an odd friend like me. And so my thoughts had rested for almost fifty years.

Time is a strange magic. Just last week I heard from an old friend who told me that Ralph had been sent to Vietnam at about the time I lost him—and that when he came home from his tour of duty, he committed suicide.

"Oh, Ralph, how far inside was far enough?" I ask myself, so very many years after. "Did you fit in at last? Were you accepted? Did you have scores of laughing friends and more invitations than you could accept? I hope you *made it in,* as you used to say, *all the way inside where it is safe,* and that it was worth it."

But something, *something* had been wrong. At some level I couldn't fathom, Ralph had felt evil even before Vietnam. I will always wonder what happened to him there. Or perhaps I should be wondering if it was the old familiar evil that overcame him.

A few days after receiving this news, I was unpacking a box of books that had been in storage for years, and I found a thin leather-bound volume, *The Rubaiyat of Omar Khayyam.* A drift of dried stems and flowers fell from the pages into my hand, fuzzy stems and tiny purple flowers.

Though my hair has turned gray, I am still wildflower girl, and now I know the flower's name. I told it to myself as I gathered the fragments and dropped them gently back into the book. "*Astragalus purshii,*" I whispered. "You are *astragalus purshii.*" From years as a field biologist, I know this little plant well. As I write, it is April here on Antelope Hill, and Pursh's astragalus is blooming in the sagebrush on the south-facing slope where I live, its soft fernlike leaves and small bonneted flowers pressed close to the desert floor to keep away from the harsh spring winds.

I think of that long-ago April day and the four friends, yellowbells blooming under the sagebrush, the songs of the meadowlarks, the wind warm and clean, the squat outline of the old safe in the bottom of the rift, the stone bowls of pure white sand, and of Ralph's face cloudless with happiness, leaning down over the canyon wall calling my name, the tiny purple flowers in his hand.

A year later, I went back to search the cleft for the gold, but I couldn't find the sharp black canyon. The rift in the desert was not where I thought it to be. But the day itself remains, unforgotten. Ralph and his memory are safe with me.

The Ghosts of North Fork

Of all Wood River's tributaries, the North Fork is coldest, flowing from a cold canyon in a cold-wintered land, pouring the ice of its heart into the main fork between steep, dark ridges.

The North Fork comes clean down the pale, washed stones of its bed, too chill to support many trout. Even on a summer day, the sunlight falls on the water of the North Fork for only a few brief hours before mountain shadow displaces it to the tops of the aspens, then to the spearheads of Douglas-fir climbing up the east ridge.

As a young girl, I knew North Fork Canyon because my father had a mine there. The mine was old, patented. Dad had not made the tunnels. They were fifty years old at least when he came by the place. The upper tunnel was hardrock and dry, but branching into two at once, so you were afraid to creep in very far; the green, fir-soft oval of the entrance shifted and winked out as soon as you chose the left or the right branch.

The lower tunnel was more inviting, being situated as it was hard by the dynamite shed and framed by graceful young firs curving away from the entrance timbers, which had been there before the trees. No hardrock here, not for more than a hundred feet in. The earth around the timbers was padded with cabochons of bright moss, emerald and topaz and peridot and garnet, and between the ore-cart rails, water ran ankle-deep, pitted by droplets falling from the sodden timbers.

Dad hadn't made the tunnels, but he shored them up, repaired the rails, beat out the dents in the old ore cart, got himself a carbide headlamp, and mined. Or more properly, he explored, for the North Fork claim never paid off.

Dad was wise to ore. He could read silver into the way things folded and cracked. I felt that he could smell the now-barren paths where gold had withdrawn from empty veins and could follow it to where it had loded up in some fat stope. Yes, he could, and proved it later, buying and selling old mines such as this one until he was able to retire early. But North Fork was the first, his teacher, great cracked shale mountain with miles of tunnels and shafts unaccountably opening here and there on slopes where there were no roads or even paths—here drowned in water, there laced with the bright desirable sparkle of galena ore.

Dad would spend his weeknights and days off in the mine, and I would go with him and wander about the canyon alone, for it was considered too dangerous for me to go into the tunnels.

To other canyons where he took me, I might bring toys—my bears or the little plastic horses. But I never brought toys to North Fork. There I mined solitude and piled up loneliness.

Dad caught trout in the North Fork and brought them in buckets to the mine-swamp's sterile ponds, where they grew slowly and their numbers gradually increased. I caught my first fish there.

I found salamanders in the dim, moss-cushioned mouth of the lower tunnel, themselves living veins of gold seeming to be born of the mine, for I found them nowhere else. The swamp bred grasshoppers unlike any I saw at home. North Fork had none of the common brown fliers. These were small cone-headed jumpers, striped green and cream and maroon. Even the butterflies were different, all shade-colored, brown and rust like fallen fir-needles, dappled silver like ore from the mine.

And I was different. The chill of the canyon wrapped about my shoulders and followed me to school. How could I explain salamanders to children who had never seen one and didn't care, who looked at me and thought, "You are talking about things that can't be understood and don't matter." How could I explain the ruby moss, the carnelian eyes of the butterflies, the death-camas lilies, the great draught and drain of cold air sluicing and singing down the riverbed when the sun caught in the ridgetop firs and set like death in a livid sky? These were, then, my secrets. The canyon made me private as I grew and learned.

After a few years, Dad found other mines and let North Fork go; but, older, I could come back alone, on horseback, no longer dependent upon Dad for the times when I could visit the canyon. North Fork was eight miles from home, too long a walk for a child on foot to go and return in the same day, but my horse could manage the trip with hours to spare.

I brought my dreams to North Fork and said them out, riding up the road across the sage flat, clopping across the bridges, sitting on the folded moss-edge of the swamp, watching the trickles of black water taking them out into the trembling bog where I dared not walk after them. I told out my dreams very carefully in the pallid sun, alone.

It came to me that I feared the canyon. I felt dogged by an invisible rider. I'd gallop down the road, wheel my horse aside in the shade of an abandoned cabin, and peer around a corner back down the road. I'd step, breathing hard, behind a fat aspen in the upper beaver swamp and listen for the suck of a foot pulling up or a little splash made by someone just out of sight behind the willows. I brought my rifle and fired a dozen shots into a bare hillside. Still the feeling persisted: someone follows.

Nothing ever surfaced; no one appeared. I never saw so much as an unexplained shadow. But I spread out my dreams like bright quilts along the road, and when I bent to fold them

The mouth of North Fork Canyon.

up and take them home, they had changed. Yellow turned to fire, a gray patch darkened to black, clean white was cast across with blue shadows, leaves sang, trees breathed, flowers fell like rain into the swamp, and the butterflies were still strange. My dreams were alien like them, brittle dreams of frost and sagebrush coals and dark flowers and night. They were beautiful. But none of them ever came true. For a while.

The summer I was fifteen, years past the age when I had acted out my dreams, at the age when I dreamed them nonstop, desperately, I began riding with Millie. I'd known her for years, an isolated little tomboy who lived eight miles north of the rest of us, less than half a mile from the mouth of North Fork Canyon. I had never played much with Millie when we were small, though I liked her; her father never allowed her to sleep over in town. But the summer we were fifteen I could drive myself to her house and stay with her, in her little room above the house's front door, where I could look north in the morning, over the green gas pumps and across the highway, up into the blue mouth of North Fork Canyon where we would ride and dream about spending the night, about living there.

The horse she rode, a bay, was Fork; I rode my gray Tony. Millie was Jesse James. I was supposed to be Cole Younger, and we were on the run, galloping up the canyon to find a place to hole up with our loot and lose the posse. "I'm too old for this," I thought at first. "I'm fifteen. This would be great if we were ten," and I tried to laugh. But Millie would have none of it. She reined in and turned her honest face toward me, preparing to be hurt, but obstinate, wanting to pretend, needing to. And she was right.

"After all, this is North Fork," I thought suddenly. Cole Younger I tried to be, and we rode at a gallop as the side canyons flashed by in dust. Murdock Creek, Sawtooth Camp, Cougar Camp. Tony was only a four-year-old, but he began to sweat. His shoulders darkened and foam flew back from the bit. He was used to exercise, but a three-mile race up a canyon at hard gallop was more than I had asked of him. Still, Millie would not stop. She turned off the road, clattered through the creek, and kept at a gallop for another mile, dodging and twisting through the lodgepole pines. She clung to the saddle like a brown Indian, and I was hard-pressed to match her skill.

Finally she said, "We'll get off and walk the horses for a while and cross the creek. The posse will have some trouble tracking us through the water, especially if it gets dark before they come to where we left the road."

A little farther on, she knelt by a muddy spring and showed me the pug marks of a mountain lion, a cat with only three toes on one of its front paws. "This is Old Slewfoot, Cole," she said. "The sheepmen have been after him for two years. Come on. If he's close, we've got to get the horses out of here."

Something shivered down the wind of the canyon and I *was* Cole. I looked back at Tony and saw him shudder and roll an eye. He blew down his nostrils and sidestepped the puma tracks, and leading him I was listening again, listening for the posse this time, though the familiar unseen stranger might be there, too.

At last Jesse climbed up a stony bank and put us back on the road. She vaulted into the saddle, kneed Fork, and became a rhythm of hooves somewhere ahead.

It was fully dark, and I followed. Fork was invisible but for the sparks, like great copper flowers, struck from his shoes by the stones in the road. They died like ashes under Tony's feet.

Finally, we made it to Mormon Camp, a huddle of gray, decrepit cabins once used as a church camp but many years abandoned. Jesse watered and picketed the horses in a near-by grassy ravine. We found an open door, collected wood, and built a fire in a cabin's stone fireplace.

We ate hot beans from a can, sitting on the floor leaning against our warm saddles. Neither of us spoke of the posse, but we kept watch, taking turns with rifle across knees, shivering in the downcanyon airs that crept in through chinks between the shrunken logs of the cabin walls. North Fork watched with us, oppressive, dark, an outlaw presence. We kept watch, but we did not expect the posse to come. We had been too clever, and North Fork was there, sentinel against the world outside, the world of reality as well as the world of dreams. The posse never came up North Fork, but often in years to come I found myself listening for it.

****

I was sixteen and it was summer—August, and so hot that even North Fork Canyon could forget the permafrost in its bones, although the fork itself, the creek, never forgot. It was the annual Old Timers' Barbecue and Picnic, and everyone who worked for the railroad and Sun Valley resort brought family, dogs, neighbors, and friends for a day of eating and singing and running around in the bright aspen-cottonwood meadow just above the confluence of North Fork with the main river. The picnic ground was on the main stream, not in North Fork Canyon itself, but the canyon breathed upon it. When I remembered, moving about the picnic tables with their red-checked oilcloths, I didn't turn my back to the canyon.

The young people paired off and slipped away into the trees. They slipped away from me. I was not one of them. I knew it and they knew it. Teenagers are not subtle. I could fish, and I could ride, I could find windflowers in the snow, and I knew all the bird songs and the sonnets of Keats, but I didn't know what they knew: how to play the game. The mark of the canyon was on me, like the patterns on the wings of the strange butterflies. It chilled me and turned them away. Youth is a time for heat.

So I turned away from the clearing. I found a path through the trees north and stumbled along it. I said a litany, a stupid prayer that I needed to say, trying to make magic out of ordinary pain, to make it heal, to make it be all right. Then the path broke free from the trees into a meadow of tall wild rye, and a gold bird hung there on a dry stem of thistle, black and gold as a salamander from the mine, ready for the wind to blow him away.

He came easily from the thistle to my finger, digging in with the dry-thorn points of his claws—not held, but holding on. The meadow opened wide, the sky arched up like a blue bowl, and he stayed on my hand while I went back to the picnic clearing. Most dreams are evanescent, unable to bear the scrutiny of others. They are dreams.

But the goldfinch was real. Everyone saw him, though likely no one remembers it now but me. And he held to me for an hour, until I took him back to the tallgrass meadow. The bird launched himself at once and flew straight as a die toward the twilight-blue mouth of North Fork Canyon, tiny promise summoned and gone.

Years later, I thought that the gold bird's promise came true. I found love, and I went up to North Fork mine and collected butterflies for him from the swamp. I pinned them and spread their tawny wings on the blocks and wrote the North Fork Canyon label and gave them to him, and for the first time in years, I felt free of the canyon, of its invisible ghosts, of the black song of the mine, of the posse and the hidden stranger.

In the years that followed, I went back occasionally, but North Fork was a canyon, one of countless others. The shadows were shadows. The wind was the wind. The abandoned cabins greyed and leaned, and moss outlined the rotting doors. Father's trout, starving and big-headed, bred in the clear pond of the mine. Nothing remained but what was there, that and the cold.

But North Fork does not let go, and its mark never fades. The gold bird had not promised that love would last. Promises from

North Fork are meant to turn cold and drain away out of reach. I should have known that the posse would come for me in the end. Cole Younger was the only member of Jesse James' gang to die an old man, freed after decades in prison. But I was not Cole Younger. He got away.

After the first dream died, there was a place for me, I thought, where I could go, and it called cold, with the voice of a thousand trees, with the song of airs blown hollow through the deep, forgotten tunnels of a mine, with the cold of Pleistocene, a cold that time forgot and left there. I was marked with the burn of frost from the canyon, I knew, cold equivalent of silverdust on butterflies' wings, and I was called. "Let the bones of gray Tony rise from his weedy grave downriver and take me back," I thought, "back to North Fork."

When my marriage died, I went to North Fork alone, and unaccountably, I was comforted.

North Fork is but a canyon, and I am only a dreamer of old dreams. That may be, but if you care to check the records of rare butterflies, of those collected in this state but once—rare silver-marked butterflies with wings like dappled shadow on dead fir needles—you will find that some were netted in North Fork Canyon, and that they were collected by me after the gold bird brought summer to the place where the ice-ghosts change dreams.

Epilogue

Not long after, the promise of the gold bird did come true and did stay, but it came late, as late as snowmelt comes to North Fork Canyon. For all unexpected and suddenly, I found another. His dreams were patterned to a different place, but one just as shadowed, just as moss-jeweled, and just as strange. As soon as I knew that Scott was the one, I brought him to North Fork, and found that the magic was still there after all, deep and chill and familiar.

As the years have come and gone, we have a tradition. After Halloween, Scott and I visit North Fork Canyon. We leave a jack o' lantern on a white boulder between the black swamp and the clear pool where the descendants of Father's trout still swim, an offering to the old spirits of North Fork Canyon. Every year, the spirits take the offering, for when we return to the boulder, the pumpkin has gone. It's likely that the pumpkin is welcome forage for the deer. But we like to think that Jack becomes one of the spirits of the place, and there are many.

When it is time, we will answer the final cold call of North Fork Canyon.

About the Author
Dana Stewart Quinney

I grew up in Ketchum, Idaho, enchanted by wildflowers and the small lives of wild things, taught to fly fish by my father, a master. After college, I married and, among other things, worked as a scientific illustrator, a field research technician, a golf-cart mechanic, a high school teacher, a college instructor, co-leader of college field biology expeditions, and for years was the biologist for the Idaho Army National Guard, ending up as Natural and Cultural Resources Manager for the State of Idaho Military division. But titles don't tell much. Here are some of the things that made up my life: watching clownfish lay eggs on the Great Barrier Reef; documenting a species of intertidal ants in Mexico; planting thousands of acres of native plants after wildfires; discovering a predatory new species of fairy shrimp; watching arctic foxes and their kits foraging along the Arctic Sea; discovering the life cycle of a rare white flower; learning the mountains and hills, the deserts and canyons of the West. And writing.

Always writing.

Note: Several names in these stories have been changed.